WHY JENNY CAN'T LEAD

UNDERSTANDING THE MALE DOMINANT SYSTEM

JINX MELIA & PAULINE LYTTLE

Published by:
Operational Politics, Inc.

Distributed by:
COMMUNICATION CREATIVITY
P.O. Box 213
Saguache, Colorado 81149

Although the authors and publisher have made every effort to ensure the accuracy and completeness of the information contained in this book, we assume no responsibility for errors, inaccuracies, omissions, or any inconsistency herein. Any slights of people or organizations are unintentional. Readers should use their own judgment for specific applications to their individual problems.

Library of Congress Cataloging-in-Publication Data

Melia, Jinx.
Why Jenny Can't Lead

   1. Women executives.   2. Power (Social sciences)
3. Sex role.   4. Women in politics.   I. Lyttle, Pauline, 1945-
II. Title
HD6054.3.M45   1985   658.4'09'024042   85-15365
ISBN 0-9614073-3-6

ATTENTION: CORPORATIONS, GOVERNMENT AGENCIES, UNIVERSITIES, AND TRAINERS: This book is available at quantity discounts on bulk purchases for educational, business, or sales promotional use. For information, please write to: Special Sales Department, Communication Creativity, P.O. Box 213, Saguache, CO 81149, or call (303) 589-8223 or (303) 655-2504.

Editing, book design, typesetting & printing coordination by
ABOUT BOOKS, INC., Saguache, CO 81149

COMMENTS

Here's what women *and men* are saying about the concepts presented in *Why Jenny Can't Lead*. Although these comments address the nationwide seminars led by the authors, they are indeed applicable to the book, which is founded on the seminar materials. These comments were selected from hundreds on file at OPI offices. They in themselves are solid testimony to the soundness of the ideas offered in this book.

"Fantastic! Now I can reach my goals knowing what they are, how to get them, what the consequences will be, and what I will need to give up to accomplish them."

Lynne Simmons, Customer Support Consultant

Metier Management Systems—Englewood, CO

"This course will definitely change my life. It has taught me new ways to view situations and has given me insight to much that goes on around me. It has given me a great deal of confidence."

Donna B. McCutcheon, Statistician
Bureau of the Census—Washington, DC

"Extremely useful, especially for men! To have an outside look at how men operate is a unique opportunity. Thank you for your perceptive insight!"

William L. Dunn, Office Manager
Alameda Optical—Lakewood, CO

"Every woman should take this course! And it should be a required course in every MBA program—no person --especially women— should go into the business world unless armed with this knowledge."

Melanie J. Rowland, Attorney
Federal Trade Commission—Seattle, WA

"This class is not for women only! I find it difficult to work with men who are politically naive. Women in the system will be a dynamic resource now and in the future."

Stephen Rolph, Construction Superintendent
Glenwood Springs, CO

"Excellent program, I feel as though I finally have an understanding of the processes which affect my daily life and the world around me."

Janice Kiracofe, Branch Manager
Central Savings & Loan—San Diego, CA

"This is without question the best seminar I have ever attended. It's hard to believe how many things are beginning to fall in place. Thank you ever so much for helping me start yet another phase of my life."

Anne Migliaccio Beer, Inventory Supervisor
Digital Equipment Corp.—Colorado Springs, CO

"Terrific Course!" To me this is an investment in my career future. This course offers a tremendous insight in "real life" politics and has had a powerful impact on my value system."

Donna R. Fell, Account Executive
Glenwood Post—Glenwood Springs, CO

"This course was an invaluable tool which I cannot wait to use. Sure wish I'd had this 20 years ago! I'll never again be the same— and hope I can in turn educate other women."

Kay Carlson
Solar Age—Santa Fe, NM

"Dynamic content!...You very well may have changed my life! Very timely...I've been out of the cave and struggling..."

Emily J. Rucker, Doctor of Chiropractic
Chiropractic Arts Center—Boulder, CO

"This course is extraordinary; it's a lot like coming of age politically—i.e., an experience that allows you to "grow up" in your perception of power and politics itself...Bravo!"

Adam Donovan, Directory Advertising Consultant
Mountain Bell Yellow Pages—Aurora, CO

DEDICATION

To Chris and Brendan
and
To Jack

To Viki,

I saw a bumper sticker
that I think fits you & me.

The meek shall inherit the earth.
The rest of us are going to the stars!

Right On!

— Suzanne
6/10/88

ACKNOWLEDGMENTS

This book, like most projects of any worth, has been influenced by a number of people who deserve mention. There are the men in our lives who have been daring and honest enough to articulate and test these ideas. John Dohring, George Gault, Terry Swaine, Bud Lyttle, Warren Wiggins, Dick Wood, Tom Dickershaid, Dick Irish, Jerry Lucas. We are also indebted to all those who confided in us privately. There are the women who tested and advanced the concepts of this book: Evelyn Day, Helen Preston, Joan Humphries, Jean Kerr, Jennie Beach, Martha Dohring, Cindy Taeuber, Paulette Licktman-Panzer, and many others who must be held in confidence. There are those who have given unconditional support, including Betsy Sheets and Randy Fox, Billi and David Ramsberger, Sherrie Flatt, Sharry Shipe, Karen Kennedy, Helise Fox, Kathy Duffy, Mike Driver, plus Eric and Diane Hanson. And finally, there are those who absolutely made it possible: Sharon Oswald, OPI's Office Director; Tom and Marilyn Ross, our editors and consultants; and Dave Flatt, our banker.

PREFACE

We are proud to present *Why Jenny Can't Lead*. It is the brainchild of Jinx Melia in whose fertile mind it was nourished and developed over many years. It has been birthed with the difficulty and pain all new ideas demand.

As co-author, I have argued long and late into the night about nuances and flow, but never about the validity of the concepts. I believe the book now stands ready to take on a new life of its own. The book itself is only a tool. But we hope that in your hands it will serve you to reach bigger and more significant goals.

Twentieth century education has done little to prepare people for the social, economic, and political challenges we face. Men and women labor together, but do not understand each other. We share the same children, but sabotage each other's strengths. We create solutions to ensure our mutual survival, but fight about both the means and the ends. As we chafe under old role restrictions, we destroy our careers and break up our families. Before we can change, we must first understand.

This book is intended to teach women about men; it may also teach men about women. It describes how political, economic, and social systems outside the family can benefit from female contributions now overlooked. It examines an age-old debate on the goals of the human condition—but in a new construct. If we are to achieve what we want as individuals, we must understand how systems control our rewards.

Through nationwide seminars, Operational Politics, Inc. has been translating for women the coded world of the Male Dominant System. The graduates of these seminars will recognize again in this guide, how very differently men and women operate and how strategies are employed. But more important, this book examines how we effect change in mutually beneficial ways.

To new readers of Operational Politics' concepts, this book stands complete and apart from our seminar work. It is the first new thinking in this decade about women, men, and the world in which they strive.

Pauline Lyttle

TABLE
OF
CONTENTS

Introduction

Discussing power is difficult and dangerous. Difficult because power changes the minute one mentions the specifics. If we were to publish the information that, in a certain town, the mayor holds titular authority—but the real mover-and-shaker is the pharmacist, whose sister is married to a state senator, the very notification of this fact would change it. The mayor would quickly try to prove he is not just a figurehead. The state senator, embarrassed by a seemingly questionable in-law relationship, would avoid the pharmacist. And the townfolk would seek to prove or disprove the information by pressuring the three individuals in one way or another.

This subject might be said to be as illusive as trying to capture an electified amoeba in a fog. The processes of power may seem to be somewhat erratic. The consequences, however, are not.

A more special problem is the danger. Everyone needs to believe he or she has and uses power very well. To assume otherwise, is to suggest personal ignorance, stupidity, and naivete. So telling you that you have misread and mishandled the power you have is bound to be insulting at some level. But more important, the people who use power well don't want the fact addressed in the light of public scrutiny for the same reasons the pharmacist and senator desire privacy.

It is impossible to put in context every action for every person who decides to judge us. It is further impossible to control their varied reactions. Open and direct disclosure doesn't work. Just ask Jimmy Carter, who directed—only to rescind later—that all cabinet meetings be aboveboard and open for public scrutiny.

When books on power are written they are usually academic and theoretical, limited to personal attributes, or depicted as history after the fact. A more effective process by which to describe power is to illustrate it with a series of verbal snapshots taken from different directions.

In this book, power is treated anecdotally. The real circumstances have been altered slightly to conceal identities. Most of the stories are parables, but the consequences of power described here are very real.

We want you to delve into your own experiences and validate what is here as relevant because it reaffirms what you already know or suspect. A thing is either true for you or it is not.

Power, as addressed here, is the Male Dominant System because men have it in this country. Until we women can understand the whys and wherefores of this fact—and become more effective power users ourselves—it will always be that way. There is work to be done before everyone enjoys equal power. It is necessary, to begin with, to provide training for women in effective operational politics in and out of organizations.

But all of this is only a beginning. The world does not really need another automobile manufacturer or insurance executive—who is only incidentally female. What it desperately does need is competent, skilled, articulate women with power bases who can influence corporate goals and humanize the Male Dominant Systems.

1.
Men, Women, and Bears

Long ago, when men and women first struggled for survival against the elements and the terrors of the world, politics was born. Specifically, gender politics was born; how men and how women perceive, react to, and approach the world and one another.

The goal was, and still is, survival. Women had some initial disadvantages of size, relative physical weakness, and the immobility of pregnancy. Wild bears roamed everywhere ready to eat or be eaten. Alone, one woman could do almost nothing to withstand the beasts. But she could create a political system to neutralize her handicaps.

BIRTH OF THE FIRST POLITICAL SYSTEM

She sought refuge in a cave to build a nest for herself and to nurture and care for her young. There she could control the environment: sheltering herself from

summer heat and winter snows; and maintaining a fire
to give warmth and light. And she could hide from the
bear.

It was not enough, of course. Occasional animals
found their way into the cave. If one attacked her, the
woman would die. And if it did not, she might die
anyway without the meat. So she invited a male into
her cave who could not only defend her against these
intruders, but also hunt them for food. In return for his
help, she offered sex, children, a warm cave and cooked
bear meat. Once in a while, other women joined her in
the cave, but this was worrisome for sometimes when
they left, the bear hunter left with them. And when the
hunter brought back only a limited supply of meat, the
women would have to fight one another for it.
Ocassionaly men would enter the cave, not to trade
protection, but to pillage and rape. Some women came
in to steal the bear fighters. It became an important
element in female survival to limit entry into her
world to those who demonstrated their interest in her
well-being.

Thus slowly and deliberately, cavewomen instituted
a sociopolitical system most beneficial to themselves
and their young. It was based on three major factors: a
limited environment through which they could
maintain control over the elements, animals, and
events; exclusion from the cave anyone they found
threatening; and bartered protection by males.

This female political system has been most readily
demonstrated in marriage rituals, nurturing, women's
roles, female jealousy, sexual monogamy, one-to-one
relationships, and other aspects of feminine society
noticeable throughout all of history and across all
cultures.

It trades heavily in the comfort of the hearth, creating an emotional security to match the physical and economic safety provided by the males. It depends largely upon service-for-protection barters between individual men and women. And it has worked. We women could control our fortunes by (limited) containment of natural elements, selective association with reliable humans, and the negotiation for male protection.

Men chose to fight the bear. They were aided by a natural aggression produced by the male hormone, testosterone, and by the logical reality there was no one to do it for them.

However, the men understood they could rarely pick the circumstances, having to battle in driving rain, intense heat, or numbing cold. Also, one man was actually no more effective against the prowler than the female. But a group of men working in concert could subdue almost any animal, with some risk. Coordinating efforts produced even better results with less risk. So the males developed the skill of joining rank. When a menace threatened any one of them, the others would drop whatever they were doing to risk their own limbs and lives in his behalf. In return, they could count on similar assistance when they needed it. Hence the quid pro quo of our modern diplomacy.

This system depended upon trust, and men went to great lengths to test and prove each others' reliability. The willingness, in the face of adversity, to join rank with one another was the most valued attribute of masculinity. It left no room for cowardice, treason, quitting, or withholding support. This was true even if individual hunters argued over other problems. A man guilty of letting down his neighbor found himself abandoned when he next faced a charging bear.

Men were also individually admired for such attributes as strategic planning abilities, grace under pressure, swiftness, muscle coordination, use of weaponry, and hunting skills. Games were invented to demonstrate and develop these talents. Competition, heartily encouraged, became the means for educating young bear hunters. The best were invariably admired by the rest of the group, for the men knew as long as no one broke rank, even a singular accomplishment would benefit them all.

Within the group, individual traits were blended to create an effective team. Good teachers paired up with good trappers and good killers. Men good with clubs joined men good with knives. The tacit agreement was to barter talents.

So developed a male-oriented political system based on cooperation, competition, bargaining, and mutual goals. Male finesse depended upon resilience in responding to situations, as it was almost impossible to predict the circumstances accompanying danger or predict the individual makeup of the bear fighting team at any given moment. The goal was always clear, but the process was necessarily flexible.

Consequently the man's world required a different set of roles than the woman's. However, men did not automatically exclude women from the hunt. A female with the requisite bear fighting and team playing skills was included—even admired—provided she was not burdened by pregnancy or other dependencies. But females in general represented a problem. If they could not take care of themselves on a hunt against the beast, they hindered the effectiveness of the entire group. If they were unable to handle their end in an emergency, they would require protection at the expense of other hunters.

The men agreed to protect those who could not defend themselves, such as women, the young, elderly, infirm, and injured. With some, the need for protection was obvious; not so with others. Men were suspicious of other men feigning illness or injury as a cover for cowardice or ineptitude. They argued among themselves from time to time as to the extent, shape, and recipients of such protection. But the men agreed on one thing. If they protected others, they had the undeniable right to determine when, where, and how protection would be provided. Further, they had the right to the first and best parts of any bear they killed.

And so it has been with gender-oriented political systems over the centuries. Women were largely excluded from the male system. But the reverse was not true, for female survival depended upon interaction with males. And males, of course, wanted females. Since women controlled the politics inside the caves, the men largely acquiesced within the caves. They dealt with women and female political systems with the same agility and resilience they employed elsewhere. Because we were intent upon controlling our environment, the males accommodated our needs to do so, even if it meant telling us only what we wanted to hear. Eventually, this led the men to adopt and support a double standard of behavior for themselves, they came to believe women were unable or unwilling to deal with the ambiguity of an uncontrolled environment.

So while the males assured the females that feminine systems were as sacred as their own, they competed among themselves to see who could get the

most attractive females to make the best clubs, cook
the most nourishing meals, and provide the best sex.
They exploited the female system of exclusion,
dependency, and control, which was relatively easy to
do because of the limited environment. Men began, for
example, to make laws which served female needs for
security, but enforced them discriminately according to
their own priorities. Women, isolated from the male
world, were largely unaware of the manipulative use of
regulatory power, and came to believe only "bad"
people broke the rules.

Men also traded on women's basic dependency.
When a female lost her mate, she required another for
survival and enticed a man from another's cave to her
own. The female dependency gave the men additional
leverage within the cave, which many of them used to
get more sex and better services. The males felt
perfectly justified in this behavior, since they did,
indeed, provide protection, and did, indeed, bring
home the meat.

Eventually, male protection came to be looked upon
by women as a divine right. Men saw it as a sign of
ownership. In the course of time, the right of female
ownership by men became so rooted that generations
later, the Judeo-Christian Bible elevated it to moral
law. The men protected the women from other men,
even as they protected both men and women from the
bears. Only the female politics of exclusivity protected
women from other women.

MODERN CAVE MENTALITY

Now it is late into the twentieth century: good male
bear fighters are hard to find and we women have long

grown tired of leftover bear meat. We have decided to fight the beast for ourselves. The difficulty is too many of us are still living in an extended cave. Too many women still believe we can control and influence circumstances the same as when our environment was contained. We expect the same male protection as we once enjoyed, only now instead of our husbands, we look to bosses and legislators. True, we expect to pay for this protection through work and taxes, but we expect it. We still cling to the emotional comfort of restricting our relationships to those whose values we accept.

The typical woman of the mid-eighties, through roles and rules, tries to control the environment in and out of the home. Many of us believe, for example, we can control the availability, the conditions, and payoff of female employment through legislation, creating a world in which there will always be well paid, enjoyable work for everyone. We disregard economic disruptions, natural disasters, supply and demand, decreases or increases in population, and other economic factors.

Furthermore, if we expend a great deal of effort and do what we're told, we expect to have security, challenge, comfort, ego satisfaction, and all the other things we could arrange for ourselves in the home. We expect it simply because we want it so. As cavewomen we could, to an extent, banish cold and create warmth, eliminate unwanted elements, and ignore the bears roaming outside. A hunter may have to sleep on the ground and eat on the run; but we could invent sheets and china and pretend this was the only way to live.

In today's man's environment, we want to be coal miners without dirt, soldiers without violence, and employees without discomfort or risk. We believe we

have these inalienable rights and expect the Male
Dominant System to provide them for us. We believe
they will provide them by making and enforcing rules,
even though astute men realize rules are only another
variation of the old bear fighting clubs, and as such are
only as effective as the person who uses them.
Nevertheless, our reliance on rules is so deeply
ingrained we even think—although our limited
experience suggests otherwise—that through tough
laws on sexual harassment, rape, and wife abuse, we
can control men.

We still insist on unilateral male protection. We
expect our bosses to provide us with meaningful jobs,
security, and good pay. We do not expect, however, to
provide those same bosses with the same kind of
protection. We do not join rank in their behalf, put our
jobs on the line when theirs are, or push for their
increased earnings while they are pushing for ours.
We're ambivalent about female bosses. In the recesses
of our guts, we recognize that the vast majority of
women in the ranks of the Male Dominant System
serve at the whim of the men behind them, without
any real power of their own. Thus we cannot count on
their protection, so we tend to ignore them, challenge
their authority, or compete to take their places.

We cling to the emotional comfort of restricting our
relationships to those whose values we accept. We still
practice exclusion, exiling from our groups, activities,
and politics those with whom we disagree. Anyone
who has ever belonged to a women's organization
knows just how exclusionary we can be. Joining ranks
is not in the general female repertoire. We don't do it
with men, and we especially don't do it with women.
While men consider it a mortal sin, in effect, to leave

another to the bear just because the two disagree over ownership of the nearest vegetable patch, women are more apt to consider it immoral not to put one's principles above the well-being of opponents.

New as we are to this game, we sometimes have difficulty recognizing the bear. The National Organization for Women, and similar groups supposedly dedicated to the furtherance of women bear fighters, actively worked *against* the 1980 re-election of former Representative Margaret Heckler—even though she had introduced the Equal Rights Amendment into Congress and fought long and hard to make it law. Her sin was that she did not also share NOW's views on abortion. The feminists turned their spears on an ally and felt virtuous doing it. Political protection is largely a male-to-female or male-to-male reality.

It is easy to understand why established men neither understand nor trust us. We vehemently demand to be treated as equal beings, but to them an equal is one who creates her own skills, safety devices, and weapons to use in mutual protection of others. Those who require protection are, if not inferior, only the recipients of charity. And here we are, not only expecting the same protection we've always enjoyed without any recognition of our obligation to provide the same, but also demanding the right to determine the extent to which protection is offered and by whom.

The outside world does not respond favorably to female political systems. In fact, successful men accommodate the world, rather than expecting the world to accommodate them. While smart males adapt office politics in response to an environment over which they have little control, we still talk about creating a system of office politics which suits our priorities, as though environmental realities were irrelevant.

Many men are still accommodating female perceptions by passing the laws we demand, by verbalizing support for female initiatives such as the ERA, and by playing "ain't it awful" with us. Liberal men, in particular, find us useful in undermining conservative ideologies to which they object.

In competition against the conservative faction, we have become a useful ally. What we fail to realize is liberal and conservative men automatically join hands, in matters of danger and urgency. They simply cast us aside when we become hindrances in battle. Men pass our equal pay employment laws and beat each other over the head with them, but in economic crises such as the recession accompanying Reagan's early years as president, men joined rank quickly and tossed Affirmative Action right out the window.

It is not just opportunistic cynicism which motivates men to use us as they do. Their long training in resilience, and our longstanding applause of male accommodation injects us both with a sense of "winning" which is often mistaken as justice and fairness.

A worrisome problem for the male establishment is, in bowing to the female perception that men and women are alike, they no longer maintain many of the male rituals which provided bear fighting training for young men. Traditional rites of passage have lost their respectability. No longer do the Boy Scouts encourage young boys to imitate male prowess. No longer are pretty women openly discussed as prizes. Often male youths share the same perceptions as their mothers and girlfriends until the first time they actually meet a bear. Some never figure it out. The growing crisis, only whispered about in organizational culture, is the growing lack of good male bear fighters.

TRAINING NEW BEAR FIGHTERS

The increasing feminization of young men is a phenomenon only beginning to rise to a conscious level. The old guard, reared with World War II bear fighting values, is increasingly concerned it can no longer clone itself. Management consultants who purport to know the solution are themselves usually men who can recognize and enjoy a good bear fight when they see one. So they have turned their attention to nurturing (called in management jargon, "employee motivation") and other skills of the cave—the attributes they don't naturally have. Books like Peters and Waterman's *In Search of Excellence* abound with female advice: "Be kind to your people and they will be kind to you." What few realize is the female system is a remarkable asset outside the cave, but only with those people who already have the old bear fighting attributes.

To teach an experienced hunter to care is to increase his repertoire—one day he may experiment with domesticating the bear. To teach caring skills to a young man who has not met his first bear may be premature. He must first learn hunting skills if he is to join the bear hunt. To teach caring skills to a woman is redundant and may be dangerous. If the young female professional is now trained in caring skills by male management specialists, she may conclude "killing by kindness" is how hunters prevail. If she unilaterally attempts to tame the bear in the middle of a hunt—just as the hunters throw their spears—everyone will suffer.

There are no training grounds for females in male politics other than what a father, husband, boyfriend, or mentor provide. There are no institutional support systems to encourage women to behave effectively in the Male Dominant System. The current seeming support for female engineers is simply another accommodation to the economic reality that businesses need more engineers. It stems from the same motivation which led society to encourage women to become teachers when baby-boom toddlers were heading for the classroom. And women of the 1980s are acting exactly like their mothers in the 1950s by acquiescing (in hopes of gaining security, status, and protection) to male economic needs.

A greater problem for women is that the female political system itself does not include the support, protection, and nurturing of one another regardless of our differing value systems. Men still have wives to count on; women do not. Men know how to negotiate and cooperate with one another even as they compete; women do not. Men know how to prevail; we do not.

The modern day bear fighting world still consists of men, women, and bears—warriors, their supporters, and adversaries. Sometimes it is hard to tell one from another. There are also the spectators: those who don't participate at all, and sit on the sidelines booing the rest of us.

Adversaries are often natural disasters like tornados and droughts. Sometimes they are human in context, like cancer or alcoholism. Occasionally, they are man-made, like bad law or despotism. And sometimes they

are other people. It is very difficult for many women—
and men—to distinguish between a ferocious bear
fighter and a ferocious bear, although one is needed to
combat the other.

Historically, warriors have usually been male.
Today, members of both sexes get to try for a place in
battle. Men still do not get to sit out the fight. Nor do
most of them want to. Testosterone, the male
hormone, sees to that.

The support role has lost favor in modern society.
This country is about to discover the consequences of
the denigration of the cave dwellers, who have been
predominantly female. No tribe can exist on the hunt
alone.

Good bear fighters are dominant, for dominating
the bear is what it is all about. The tool for dominance
is power, and power can be described as who gets to
make the decision.

The decision to kill or not to kill the bear. The
decision to obstruct the bear's intention to kill humans.
The decision to determine how to kill the bear. And
where. And when. And why. And with whom.

When power struggles arise, as they always do, it is
over who makes the decision. This is a female game,
too; it is the basis for leaving the cave. We made the
decision, got enough men to agree with us, and here we
are.

Where we are is on male turf, forced to learn male
politics, not because we want to imitate their
behaviors—but because competent men know how to
get what they want from their turf, and we don't. As
female politics reflects our response to our former
environment, so male politics reflects theirs. Outside
the cave, it is a Male Dominant System.

only powerful woman in her own right as Katherine Graham, owner of the *Washington Post*. According to the Securities and Exchange Commission, only 11 of the 6,500 full-time working directors and officers of major U.S. corporations are women. These are the people who control this country's business.

Among those who make our laws, there are two female senators out of 50 and 21 women among 435 men in the House of Representatives. There is one female Supreme Court justice. But the numbers don't matter nearly so much as the reality that these women, and others like them, derive their authority and status from the men around them, much like the wives of the famous and the powerful. Men make the decisions which govern our lives. The Male Dominant System is so well ensconced it doesn't make any difference how many token women are seated with the august, because men can—and do—eliminate them whenever they cease to be useful. And because men control the system, they create the priorities primarily to benefit themselves. Token women maintain power only as long as they support and enforce male priorities.

An occasional female commands power in her own right—Katharine Graham in our country, Margaret Thatcher and the late Indira Ghandi in theirs. She does so, however, by beating men at their own game. Such women are skilled in traditional male behaviors such as upsurping men's power bases and aligning themselves with powerful male allies. The Katherine Grahams of this world are indeed "real men" in the sense they develop attributes commonly ascribed to men and outdo men in their own fields. Unfortunately for the rest of us, female leaders win their positions by thinking as men think and adopting male values; thus it is as if we were being led by men, when one of these women lead us. The fact of sex becomes incidental.

SERVING AT THE WHIM OF BENEFACTORS

Geraldine Ferraro found favor with the king-makers of the Democratic Party as a talented, hardworking, good-looking, and articulate female. She was rumored to be a favorite of Tip O'Neill, Speaker of the House, which is apparently of no little consequence, since a year earlier, Ms. Ferraro was so little recognized as a powerful figure in her own right that she was omitted from *Ladies' Home Journal's* October, 1983 list of the 100 Most Influential Women in the U.S.

Mary Crisp is also talented, hardworking, good-looking, and articulate. She labored with commitment and dedication for many years in the Republican party ranks before the men in power picked her to become the Co-Chair of the Republican National Committee in 1976. Yet she was summarily dismissed before the 1980 Republican convention because she and then-candidate Ronald Reagan found the organization wasn't big enough for both of them.

Midge Costanza was another woman elevated from relative obscurity to a position of national prominence because she was talented, hardworking, good-looking, and articulate. Newly elected President Jimmy Carter elevated Costanza, then Vice-Mayor of Rochester, New York, to the White House. She served as the Special Assistant to the President for Public Liason, until she developed the unfortunate tendancy of calling a press conference whenever she disagreed with him. Constanza was then dismissed and has vanished from the ranks of power players.

Mary Cunningham, an honors graduate from Harvard Business School, started her corporate rise as an executive assistant to Bill Agee, then president of Bendix Corporation. This talented, hardworking, good-looking, articulate woman became a Bendix vice-president in 14 months. But she was forced out of her position when Agee made the extraordinary move of announcing, at a company meeting to which a reporter had been invited, that he and Cunningham were *not* sleeping together.

All four of these women have a great deal in common—besides the fact they are talented, hardworking, good-looking, and articulate. They all lack the power, political astuteness, and personal acumen to play a tough man's game in a tough man's arena. They were all creations of men.

Each of these women was picked for her role by a man (or men) who found it in his interest to do so. Each maintained her position only so long as she chose to follow the goals and dictates of her benefactor. And each is without the political power base or understanding from which to grab, create, or keep control over her own future. They all served at the whim of a personal mentor, but without the bilateral power mentorship provides canny males. None of these women knew how to develop an independent political base of their own that made them equal partners in relationships with the men around them.

Token females have several functions: 1) to follow the dictates of men, and by so doing extend male power; 2) to give other women in the organization a perception of sexual inclusion at the top (thereby gaining for the organization the loyalty, cooperation, and hard work of female employees); 3) to try out new ideas and policies which may backfire, thus protecting the male supremacy; and 4) to create an expendable executive resource whose skills and talents may be an asset to the organization today—and disposable tomorrow.

FEMALE POWER BASES

Historically women have enjoyed several, mostly limited, bases of power under men. The first is for the exceptional woman who is a bear fighter in her own right—who can hold her own against all comers, who expects and gives no quarter. She leads just as men do, sharing their skills and priorities. For her, gender is irrelevant.

Then there is the occasional female who acts as second in command—the trusted lieutenant to the male generalship. She is usually superb at implementing another's policies, marketing someone else's ideas, and creating loyalty for her commander. Men often favor women for this position, since men have a tendency to create their own armies and personal power. Males are likely to eventually challenge the leadership; women are likely to stay in second place. The female lieutenant, like the lady bear fighter, derives power by adopting males goals and behavior. Neither is the same as the token, who is usually put to work doing nonessential work without any real decision-making authority.

Other women, like Nancy Reagan, know their places and polish them to perfection for personal reward and the advantage of the men and the system they nurture. In any Male Dominant System, a number of women with well-turned ankles and well-bred

manners are showcased; bright women quickly figure
out how to gain personal power and prestige through
this function, occasionally implementing far-reaching
objectives.

Jane Fonda, for one, has learned how much more
effective is her active body than her active mind. Linda
Evans and Joan Collins of the "Dynasty" television
series have done more to create opportunities for
middle-aged women than NOW could ever hope to
accomplish. Elizabeth Dole, Secretary of Transporta-
tion, has added a new perspective to marriage, by
combining her own competence in the male world
with her husband's political base, thus creating a new
opportunity for power which enhances them both.

The vast majority of women, however, find
themselves on the fringes, doing work no one else
wants to do, living in conditions which are sometimes
impossible, continually checking but never betting
their hand. These are the unhappy waitresses and store
clerks, the unwilling wives and mothers, the forever
sad and angry feminists. Betty Friedan calls them the
women of "quiet desperation." They know life doesn't
have to be this way, but haven't figured out how to
change it. Old habits are like cobwebs which have
turned into cables, imprisoning them in mediocrity.

These are the women who rush into careers in law
or civil engineering hoping male approval will give
them the recognition and sense of self-worth they so
badly want. These are the women who, against their
better judgment, leave the hearth for unsatisfying
employment in hopes of earning enough money to buy
the material items which will support their mates'
faltering egos, wanting to believe "the economy"
requires this. These are the women who seek

fullfillment in marriage and, finding none, condemn their spouses, marriage, monogamy, promiscuity, heterosexuality, womanhood, parenthood, home-making, employment, and all of sexuality for their dissatisfaction. They buy every self-help book and take every self-help course seeking the "answer," so everything will be fine. These are the women who turn to pills, alcohol, sex, violence, or resignation in a desperate search for purpose. These are the women (almost every woman we've ever met) who internalize their failures, who whisper to themselves at inopportune moments, "What is wrong with me? Why haven't I figured this out?"

Yet we don't have to be this way. If we learn how to overcome our internal barriers, we can comprehend the Male Dominant System and work with it.

3.
Internal
Barriers

Several times in the past century, women have marched out of the cave ready to face our destiny. World War I gave us our initial opportunity to experience factory life. Soon after, we won the right to vote. But almost immediately we clashed head-on with a bear of unimaginable ferocity—the Great Depression. Few of us—man, woman, or child—was a match for that beast, and those of us who could retreat to the safety of the cave gratefully acknowledged the mercy of an almighty God.

World War II brought us forth again, in patriotic fervor against another kind of bear. The hunt was concentrated in Europe and Asia. We worked passionately to supply our hunters with the weapons for victory.

Twenty years ago we stepped out again, this time buoyed by technological advances which allowed us, for the first time in history, motherhood by choice. We were accompanied by the maturing of the world's largest baby boom—thousands upon thousands of young people seeking first employment—right alongside their mothers.

WOMEN BECOME PART OF THE WORK FORCE

This circumstance was a bonanza for business. Industry quite rightly cherishes entry level employees, particularly those with brand new technical or professional degrees, because they tend to know all the latest advancements, which their elders do not. And they work for relatively low salaries, which again their elders, with-three-children-ready-for-college-and-a-maturing-mortgage, do not. Middle-aged women, with years of nonqualifying homemaking experience to their credit, could be paid just like the kids, offsetting the demons of inflation, union contracts, and seniority pay. Younger women competed against their male peers, judged by criteria with which few women were familiar. But it was also the time of civil rights sensitivity, and the feminist issues were able to piggyback on the Black Movement. White men turned in our direction with newfound sensitivity and old resilience. They decided to accommodate our demands for equality. They gave us all a seat at the poker table. That is all they gave us. The rest of the so-called feminist gains have been mostly female-accommodating illusions ever since.

To the males in power, a seat at the table was equality, an opportunity to show what we had, with the same risks and responsibility men enjoyed. For many women, it was not enough. We demanded poker instructions, a donated stake, and the guarantee of a win every third hand. Some of us have achieved them all and more, proud we can play the game on our own terms. But every competent male—and female—knows in his or her heart of hearts a guaranteed win and a donated stake is not poker.

There are essentially two political games being played today—his poker (also known as football, war, and bear fighting in all its sundry forms), and tokenism/accomodation which is played safely on the sidelines. While women are being sidelined, it is not necessarily men who are sidelining us. Many of them sincerely want our assistance in the high stakes game of business, politics, and industry. And many others are sabotaging us without knowing it. More often, we unconsciously sideline ourselves. This is not just a power struggle, but a complex communication problem.

RECOGNIZING DIFFERING GENDER VOCABULARIES

One difficulty is men and women use the same vocabulary to describe different phenomena. We call two different games "poker," two different realities "equality," two different modalities "alikeness." We use the *identical words* and phrases, yet we are describing *totally different* constructs, priorities, values, concepts, and perceptions.

Erik Erikson pointed out there are 360 ways to view an elephant, and every person standing in a circle around the animal sees only a small part of the whole, but each has "the truth." Yet a person on the north side can speak quite rationally about a "long thing hanging down, swaying freely," to a person on the south side, who also sees a "long thing hanging down, swaying freely." They don't know each is describing a very different part of the beast's anatomy, used for very different functions, with very different consequences to the observer.

So it is in the organizational world. Women seek instruction from male management. We ask, "What attributes do you value most in young men and women coming behind you?" Consistently, they respond, "Professionalism, teamwork, initiative, competence." We nod knowingly, demonstrate the very best of these skills to our male superiors, who nod back approvingly—and promote others.

The problem is we're still trying to make sense of the male world as though it were an extended cave; we apply female politics to male reality. If the world does not fit our perceptions, then we shall, we think, change the world. We look at male skills as we look at our own: tools for control. When men tell us they value professionalism, we perceive they are talking about an external factor which will control others' opinion of our worth to them. We rush to the stores to change our images, so we will have the professional look. We gather around us degrees, certifications, awards. We copy what we perceive our male peers are doing: if they bring work home at night, we do too. Our definition of "professionalism" signifies a look, an ambience, a mode of behavior, a style.

Savvy men have something very different in mind. The male pinstripe suit serves the same function as the football jersey or military uniform. It replaces individuality with a tribal identity so each man acts in coordinated concert with the rest of the team. Together they become an impenetrable unit, sharing the same goals, values, and leader; sacrificing individuality to participate in a tribal mindset identifiable by a united look, ambience, mode of behavior, and priority.

That kind of oneness is alien to women's experience. Our salvation has always depended upon our individuality. We needed to be better looking, better acting, or better bred than other females to win the favor of men, and the accompanying safety and security. Furthermore, in our caves, homes, and communities, *we* individually determined the values, priorities, and goals. We still want to make those judgments for ourselves. So though we dress and act like "professionals," most of us work diligently to overcome uniformity by seeking individual recognition and independent reward. The more we aspire to be professional, the more we signify our reluctance to establish a team consciousness. The ruling males don't know we do this any more than we are conscious of it. They only know, for all our appearances, we are generally unreliable team players by their definition.

"Initiative" causes us similar grief. Female history is filled with diligence and perseverance. We often labor heroically in spite of sickness, even danger. But we have always tried to control danger through male protection. To us, it doesn't make sense to knowingly *seek* a dangerous mode of action when it can be avoided. So we fail to see the risk men inherently expect with "initiative;" we do not understand the male who does only his job, however well he does it, lacks initiative. That attribute is reserved for those who go beyond their authorized duties, step past their prescribed roles, and put aside traditional formulas in order to reach the organizational goals—often at great personal risk to themselves. If they fail, they expect to pay the penalty—dismissal, demotion, or even death.

It was never our reality to behave in this manner.
Our dependency required conformance and obedience
to the wishes of the male tribal leadership. It still does.
A kind of craziness develops: males, unified by team
identity can act individually within the group, or even
act so independently as to form a group of their own.
Women, dependent as we are upon conformity, insist
on individually expressing this conformity even as we
demand conformance by all.

For example, if it is traditional within an
organization to win a certain promotion by presenting
a proposal at an annual meeting, we women will strive
to present the most individualistic and creative
document imaginable. Most of us would be horrified if
the promotion went to someone who demonstrated
the worth of his ideas without having to present a
paper at all. We wouldn't call it "initiative," but
"unfairness."

In the end, men proficient in their system deem us
"incompetent," unable to participate effectively in
whatever corporate battle is at hand. And once more
we misunderstand because our definiton of "competence" is based on technical and professional skills, not
on political ones.

The communication gap cannot be easily resolved,
particularly in organizational or management terms.
Older men use a different mode and code from the
typical female's. Young men can access both male and
female codes, but lack the experience to differentiate
between them. Women want security, the assurance
there are rules—accompanied by firm guarantees—
that lead to success. The outstanding, of course, derive
for themselves exceptional opportunity and reward.

It is not just accommodation that encourages men to give us apparent approval when we act incomprehensibly to them. Men are socialized to protect us; our political incompetency is a signal that we, for all our protests, still require their protection. They are still needed.

In addition, almost everyone of both sexes, relishes the willingness of another human being to take instructions, do the grunt work, and implement policy without argument. If everyone needs a "wife," many men find them at the office: secretaries, technical employees, professionals eager to understand and follow their rules.

If we are to make use of the unmistakable opportunity awaiting us in the spheres of business, commerce, politics, and industry, we must first understand *what* shades our perceptions and determines our complex ideas. Our biology and experiences forces (and enables) us to bring to the man's world a whole new dimension. If we can step back and look at the female experience in general terms, we can begin to discover for ourselves our political realities.

OUR NEED FOR APPROVAL

Women seek, demand, and require male approval. It is as basic to American women as breathing and as old as we are. We share a strong, overriding need for approval and a corresponding fear of disapproval. This is not the same as the male need for admiration or respect. Female approval implies permission. We really do believe we must have the approval of others—their permission—in order to operate.

All babies are born with a strong political sense. It's often the only thing that keeps them alive. A doctor who treats deaf people said when two deaf parents had a normal hearing baby, the infant did what all the other infants in the nursery did when he got hungry: he cried. But after being home with his parents for a month or so, the baby stopped the now ineffective behavior of crying when he was hungry. Instead he increased his body movements to successfully attract his parents' attention. The doctor observed this reaction eight different times during his career. A month-old child can figure out the system to get what he needs and wants, unencumbered yet by taboos and moral codes.

As small children, we also were very good at perceiving the systems which governed our options. Before we entered school, for example, we were encouraged to go to the bathroom whenever we felt like it; once in the classroom this same behavior was unacceptable. The school system was markedly different from the home operation, but we quickly figured it out: give the teacher (or any person with authority) what she (or he) wants, she will approve, then she will reward us. She will let us erase the blackboard, carry the notes to the principal's office, sit on the coveted seat in the school bus—all high status stuff for kindergartners.

Conversely, if we incurred the disapproval of those in charge, we would be punished by being kept in at recess, put at the end of the lunch line, or brought to a conference with our parents. By the time we had been in school for two weeks, we had the system down cold. Obtain the approval of those with power, and they will reward us. Incur their disapproval, and punishment results.

For most girls, this message of approval was reinforced so often in so many ways by the time we'd been in school several years, we had internalized it in our subconsciousness. By high school, most of us would insist the world was cube shaped if that was the test answer the teacher wanted. We entered the adult world with perception intact, assuming we only had to get the approval of authority in order to receive our due rewards.

Little boys had different training. They, too, understood differing systems required differing modes of behavior. But they received other, conflicting messages about systems. For example, they were told—as we little girls were—if they got dirty, they'd be punished. And both little girls and boys were punished if they got dirty before church on Sunday. But whereas Sally would also be punished if she played in the mud on Wednesday, Tommy would get rewarded with ice cream sodas because he had done his playing on the muddy football field.

Children were told by their mothers if they hit the child next door, they'd be sent to bed without supper. When *she* hit the child next door, she was sent to bed without supper by mom with a lecture from dad; when *he* hit the child next door he was sent to bed without supper by mom. But dad said, "Did you get him? Let me show you how to do it next time."

These double standard messages created in young males the perception that gaining rewards through approval and obedience was only one of a number of alternatives available to them in reaching their goals. Some smart child figured out if he really wanted to erase the blackboard, he could wait until the teacher was out of the room and eliminate the middleman altogether. Thus does resilience begin.

Many of us have learned, one way or another, this system of approval and reward does not work outside of childhood, academia, and marriage. But most of us also decided it was our fault. Looking inward instead of at the operation around us, we try harder to play the wrong game better, while astute men perceive that the adult male world operates on filling needs instead of gaining approval.

By adulthood, too many women are addicted to approval. It pervades our goals, thoughts, and actions. This need displays itself in many ways. We spend an inordinate amount of time and energy in approving and disapproving issues and people—especially other women. (We know where our bread is not buttered and where overt criticism is safe.) We think it matters to men whether or not we approve of someone, and we cannot understand people like past Secretary of the Interior, James Watt, who seemed to thrive on disapproval.

We also are extremely diligent about seeking acceptance from bosses, husbands, and others we perceive to be in control of our fortunes. When we receive our hard earned approval, we then relax and wait for the reward which was inevitable in school. But it rarely comes. We are disappointed. We are frustrated. We try harder to obtain approval, get it, then wait once more. We have yet to learn approval is its own reward. Eventually we begin to feel someone is cheating us out of our just desserts. We determine our bosses are biased against females, our husbands are insensitive cads, authority is unfriendly. And we become more firmly convinced we personally must be doing something wrong; why else wouldn't we be rewarded as in the past?

As always, control rather than resilience is the standard for females. It is the hallmark of "femininity." A noticeable example of this is the difference between "female" etiquette which is based on rather rigid rules of practice, and "male" diplomacy which is far more responsive to the individual situations and changing circumstances.

THE UNSPOKEN MAYBE

That same male diplomacy enables men to accommodate us when we seek security. What we get is certitude's freedom from doubt: answers, rights and wrongs, absolutes. Men rarely talk to us of estimates, appraisals, possibilities. ("I believe if you do a good job for me, I'll probably promote you within the next several years.") We want a specific guarantee. ("If you meet the qualifications for the job, as outlined in the personnel file, I'll promote you within two to six months after the job is vacated.")

This is not deception from the male point of view. Experts often start from absolutes as a useful way to resolve a particular problem. They pronounce, for example, every driver must come to a complete stop at all stop signs. They find it unnecessary to add the rule doesn't apply if the brakes on the car are not working, an avalanche is about to descend upon the road, a sniper is hidden in nearby bushes, or a passenger in the automobile is close to death. Male rules allow for contingencies and extenuating circumstances. That is why judges, juries, and parole boards exist.

Too often, we women don't hear the "maybe" in:

"You can always get a job teaching." "We need good engineers." "The people who work hard around here move up." "You can't go wrong with this stock." "You must have a college education in order to get a decent job." "You must put it in writing." "I will love you forever."

Or in these: "Housewives have no marketable skills." "Women are too emotional." "Whatever you do, don't cry on the job." "You're paid only what you are worth." "It's unprofessional not to charge for your services." "You should always pay when you invite a man to a business lunch." "Raising children is women's work."

Most such political pronouncements are made by people who sincerely believe them because those beliefs have been useful to them personally. Solidifying them into a political system also benefits those who create and manipulate the system. Leaving the "maybe" unsaid allows powerful men to differentiate between those who are like themselves -- and the powerless rest of us who can be used.

Unfamiliar as women are with the organizational world, and inexperienced as we are with spoken male "maybes," we hear only the certitude. Now we have the rules. Now we know what to do.

Organizational managers know very well blind obedience is valuable only in computers and bottom level employees. Movement upon the managerial ladder requires resilience and risk. Upward mobility in these uncertain times goes to those who create more effective new guidelines, not to those who follow the old. But what can we do? We start somewhere at the bottom and diligently seek male acclaim by rigidly following their rules. Senior males readily provide approval, for approval has become the currency which keeps women doing grunt work. Men make the rules and we win favor by following them. Approval in this case, however, is the only reward.

Jinx's son, Chris, at the age of eight, played in a championship soccer game as a fullback. The goalie was momentarily out of action. An opponent, fullbent upon scoring a goal, furiously dribbled the ball down the field. Chris was the only available defender. He did what he was supposed to do: he tried to kick the ball out of the way. He missed. Then his eight-year-old male mind provided an alternative -- he tripped the opposing player.

Chris' team was penalized for his outrageous foul, but it also won the game. He now has a trophy on his desk that says to him, "They don't keep track of how many players you trip, only how many games you win." If, Jinx, his mother, insists it is not who wins or loses, but how you play the game that counts, Chris would have quite rightly concluded she doesn't understand his world.

Little girls never face the surprise of changing circumstances which require a complete turnaround in strategy. A football player learns quickly even the best plans run awry. The quarterback may be instructed to throw the ball to George on a given play, but if George trips and falls, the quarterback may have only two or three seconds to find an alternative play. All the while during the game, the cheerleader does exactly what she learned to do on Monday in practice. There are no circumstances under which her strategy changes. The process is everything.

The uncertainty produced by our need for security and approval requires us to focus on the process rather than the goals at hand. Goal setting, as it is discussed in modern business, is essentially a traditional male attribute. Female cave dwellers don't set concrete measurable goals. Our goals are to survive, to raise our children, to maintain our marriages, to keep our families safe and happy. There is no end in sight—or in mind. We don't measure such objectives in concrete terms; they can't be graphed on a computer like a profit:cost ratio. Attention to process is the basis of the female political system.

MEANS VS. ENDS

In the male world, this seems frivolous. Processes to men are important, but only in the context of predetermined goals. When men ask, "Does the end justify the means;" they are never in doubt there is a desirable and definable end, whatever the means.

We recently overheard a man say, "I think it's terribly important for us men to become more sensitive to our employees; it's good business." And so it is. His goal is to make money; our goal would be to be sensitive. Our goal would be good process.

The point is if women do not accommodate men by creating five year plans and spread sheets, we look frivolous and unskilled. And in their world we are. For joining the bear fight was never the sole purpose of the hunt.

The result --from our side of Erikson's elephant—is a woman who is moral, hardworking, and on the side of fair play and justice. But she is also emotionally alone in the struggle, continually misunderstood, embattled, victimized, constantly caught in double binds, and compulsively seeking the truth—which men withhold.

From the other side of the elephant, the view is different. The political gap between male and female perceptions is huge. Politic men see a self-righteous female, smug and intolerant, obstructive and naive, focused on process without discernable result, given to judgmental bitchiness, unwilling to take her licks like the rest of the guys, and demanding protection even as she screams for independence.

Men who have figured it out use women to achieve their own aims. Male politics is, most of all, resilient. Such men always prevail. They accommodate us in order to make us work for them. At the moment, there is a *semblance* of power—tokenism, ineffectual legislation, inflationary salaries justified as necessary costs, corporate pats on the back, lip service, and lots of social approval. The real poker game—where with-it men use age-old strategies for bluffing, raising, and winning—is elsewhere.

4.
Strategies

Modern day bear fights are rarely violent, although war is still considered a viable alternative to argument in every civilization on earth. Most battles today take place in the arenas of business, religion, and politics. The bear is other men, other value systems, other societies. And to train all youngsters to recognize and defeat a variety of bears is an increasing challenge. Games are still the most effective methods.

THE GAME IS THE THING

It used to be said football builds character, and from a powerful male perspective, it does. What men learn from playing or watching football would surprise even the ardent female fan. Football, poker, golf, and other male play activities are the training grounds for teaching and reinforcing power skills and attributes among men. They are also culling places. Members of the "good old boy" network identify, test, and embrace or exclude potential political players according to their shrewdness and stomach for the games.

Not understanding this almost instinctual and

largely unconscious male ritual, women demand access to the game—only to demonstrate our naivete and unsuitability to play. We often expose our uselessness in the middle of the football field or golf course. We cannot entirely blame men for refusing to play with us. As one male executive told us, he was tired of throwing the ball to a woman so she could make a touchdown, only to have her accuse him of trying to hit her with something.

Mike Royko of the *Chicago Tribune* writes of a woman playing on a coed baseball team who sued the coach and a center fielder she collided with while chasing a hit ball. Her arm was broken from negligence, she charged, because the other player had not yelled, "I've got it," and had not been instructed to do so by the coach. As ridiculous as this may seem, it is no different from the female engineer who insists upon being put into a wholly male environment and then sues her boss because the male engineers whistle at her. Nevertheless, the game is open to anyone with the desire to play. The lessons are available to all with the ability to learn.

In any football game, as in any male activity in or out of the office, the person with the ball (power) is probably going to get tackled, and not just by people who disapprove of him. In fact, the better a ball carrier he is, the more people will be out to get him. And even as he is falling to the dirt in pain, the ball carrier can admire a good play, a good tackle, and a good tackler. In fact, quarterbacks are the very best people to recognize the opposing tackles who are good enough to play for their side. If the quarterback never lets himself be vulnerable to the tackle he won't know a good player. It doesn't matter whether the quarterback or the tackle is a nice person, a personal friend, an enemy, or a member of a competing team. The only pertinent question is, "Can we use him on our side." Sharp game players, of course, know their worth and when asked, answer, "Yes, in return for which...." In games, as in life, it's each person's responsibility to take care of himself. What protection and teamwork exists is bought and paid for.

A NEW LOOK AT ACHIEVING GOALS

All male games are constructed in the same way: a goal is presented with obstacles placed between the player and the goal. The object, of course, is to eliminate or overcome the obstacles—often at great personal risk—and reach the goal. Sometimes the obstacles are human. Sometimes they're natural elements as in snow skiing. And sometimes they are arbitrary barricades such as a pole vaulter faces. The man who is revered by his peers is the one who can conquer all varieties of obstacles to reach his goals and become stronger for doing it. The man next valued by other men is the one who, defeated by an obstacle, remains undaunted. Even though bloodied, he is ready to enter the game once more.

So it is in business, politics, and war. The person of greatest value is the one who overcomes the obstacles to get the goal. (This is, by the way, what men mean by "working hard." Women often interpret "working hard" to mean putting in time.)

The employee, male or female, who complains about the obstacles and wants them eliminated is similar to the tennis player who wants to get rid of the net.

The game which interests us here is the power game, usually referred to as the activities of the "white male establishment." It is often communicated in code and not always apparent to nonplayers, but it is real, compelling, and monstrously effective. In order to understand this game, it is important to realize for a smart man it is not a game at all. One sets a definable goal, focuses on it, and tries a process by which to reach it.

An example we use a lot in the seminars we give for government and private industry, is of the four-year-old boy trying to catch a pigeon. He first called the pigeon to come to him. It didn't work. So he ran after the pigeon. That didn't work either. The third strategy he used was to try to terrorize the pigeon by screaming at it. The pigeon flew away several yards. Strategy number four seemed an attempt to hypnotise the bird. The child stared intently and deliberately. No success. The boy then took some crumbs out of his pocket and threw then upon the ground. The pigeon ambled over to the crumbs. Strategy six, the one that worked, was to hold the crumbs in the palm of his hand. The pigeon was caught.

That short procedure is all there really is to power. Set a goal, focus on it, try different strategies until reaching it. Unfortunately, many of us employ almost the opposite technique. For most women, the preferred strategy is "musterbating"—preaching to others the "musts" we hold dear. We figure if we do it well enough and often enough, our audience will convert to our beliefs. Another of our ploys is to get others to musterbate with us. We write papers. We publish articles. We march. If this approach doesn't work, we change our goal. When we discern we're failing too often, we take musterbation lessons: learning to do the wrong thing better. For most of us this is easier than admitting the strategy didn't work. Instead, we think, we didn't do it well enough.

If we consider the successful pigeon routine as the cornerstone of male power, it gives us a basis for analyzing and identifying effective behavior in the male world. But remember we're talking about something dynamic; it will never be just like we describe.

It is not enough, of course, just to set goals. They must first be appropriate. It has been said women set low business aspirations. Indeed, one of the hallmarks of a poor manager, male or female, is the tendency to set small goals.

Ineffective people are rarely aware of their real goals. They may say, and even believe, they want to increase the profit of their company. But in reality they seek approval or safety or emotional comfort. It takes only a few seconds to ascertain whether these are the overriding aims of an employee. In order to determine whether a woman—or man—seeks approval, a powerful person has only to say, "I'm having lunch tomorrow with so-and-so to discuss a business matter. What can you tell me about him (or her)?"

If the employee replies, "What a jerk!" or "Marvelous human being!" the inquirer knows the other is dependent upon approval because such people believe approval and disapproval are terribly important and so indulge in it themselves. If the employee were to say instead, "So-and-so does his job." or "You should have an interesting lunch," or some other noncommital statement, the astute questioner will understand the employee does not expend energy on judging the worth of others and is probably immune to it personally.

Similarly, nonrisk-takers always give reasons why something cannot be done. "'They' won't allow it." "It'll never work." "John would never spend money that way." "We've always done it like this."

Those who seek emotional comfort betray themselves by wanting others to change without having to do it themselves. They expect the world to be more peaceful, people to be more polite, and bosses to be more understanding—without any accompanying requirement on themselves to alter their own priorities. When women leak such messages to powerful men, we give them extraordinary insight into how they can manipulate us.

Another difficulty we often have with goals is staying focused on them. Barbara, a mid-level executive at a large company, was invited by her boss to help carve up the company budget at the quarterly meeting. The other men didn't want her there. They, of course, didn't express their displeasure directly to Barbara. They waited until the meeting had begun. Then after 10 minutes or so, one of the men called her a "broad."

She reacted immediately. "How dare you talk to me that way!" All the men became solicitous. "Oh, we're so sorry. What would you like to be called...Ms., Miss, or Mrs.? What does your husband call you? Your secretary? Your children? What do they call you in the office? In the kitchen? In the bedroom?"

Barbara spent the rest of the time discussing how she wished to be addressed while the men listened solemnly. Then they went into the bathroom and carved up the budget. Now they know any time they want to deflect Barbara from her goals, they have only to call her a "broad."

It *is* hard, as men say, to remember your job is to clean the swamp when you're up to your ass in alligators. Smart men bent on deflecting women or weak men, keep a couple of the beasts around just for that purpose. (No wonder they call it a jungle out there!)

The biggest difficulty women face about goals, however, is our inability to free ourselves from impediments. Mao Tse Tung said if a person is willing to risk death, he can accomplish anything! He'll either get it or be dead. What Mao meant was the fewer goals a person has at any one time, the more likely he or she is to get them. Most of us want to be President of General Motors, popular with our friends, emotionally comfortable, challenged without risk, and totally accepted by our spouses and family all at the same time. There's no way. Women simply can't have it all. No one can. Human energy is like a flashlight. If we focus in one direction, we cannot simultaneously focus in another. We either must swing wildly from one place to another, losing perspective, or we must stand so far back to widen the beam that it loses potency in the process.

Those who overcome all the obstructions to their goals—almost to the point of obsession—usually reach them. Yes, they pay a high price for the privilege. Additionally, they're highly valued by the male power structure for their ability to do so.

The majority of human goals involve interaction with other humans, either as allies or adversaries. People either help a person or organization reach its goals, or they hinder it. Power plays invariably involve manipulating, sidelining, overcoming, or obstructing others. We all try. The white male establishment simply does it better than the rest of us.

As we said women often depend upon "musterbating". If that doesn't work, we often turn to obstructing others. This makes us feel good, because we are accomplishing something; but it doesn't get us any closer to our goals. There are more effective ways to accomplish what we want. The white male establishment maintains power because it has figured this out.

Musterbating is usually ineffective because it involves changing people's values. It's not just because we want people to do what we wish; we also want them to believe as we do. Our bent for exclusivity makes us all missionaries; if I can only allow myself to relate to those who are just like me, I have to make just like me those with whom I relate. Telling others why our way of believing is better is just another way of saying they are wrong. It's not the easiest way to encourage cooperation.

Moreover, in America, we have come to grips with our multicultural society by tenaciously holding on to our individual value systems even as we more or less agree to follow the dictates of the ruling majority. Thus most of us will follow and respect the courts, however grudgingly, as long as we don't have to agree with them. So demanding an American change his or her values is usually futile. Even a casual glance at issues such as abortion and gun control supports the above statement. When such issues are first raised, polite discussion is possible, even welcomed. But once people have made up their minds on the issue, further musterbation only widens the gap between the believers and the non-believers. It simply doesn't work.

Forceful power players rarely even try to convince or persuade others. They know it is easier to get people to cooperate if they don't attack values. It is our behavior, not our beliefs, they are after. So they have developed other strategies. Nothing works all the time, and nothing is without risk. Nevertheless, there are alternatives to failure.

BARTERING FOR WHAT WE WANT

A popular tactic employed by male power brokers is the barter. It is simply a matter of exchanging favors. I do something for you; you do something for me in return. If I fight your bear, you fight mine. The terms of the barter are determined through negotiation, either informal, such as, "I'll take you to the movies tonight, if you'll iron my shirts"—or formal, such as, "I'll get my missiles out of your neighboring country if you give up all research and experimentation in germ warfare."

Successful negotiatiors avoid values altogether when they get down to business. Instead, they barter with one another point by point. One person does a favor for another for an immediate or future favor. The person who owes the favor is obligated to repay the debt, however, whenever the person who is owed desires. The deal is struck and the obligation incurred with both parties aware of the responsibilities.

As Aristotle Onassis pointed out, a man has but one thing to sell—his word. If he owes a debt and doesn't pay off when requested, the other man will let every other power player know his debtee is not trustworthy and no one will do business with him again. Onassis lived in a world of such rarified power that he had no qualms about lending a tanker to a business associate. Contracts were often unnecessary. Trust was never a factor. Leverage mattered (and still does). Onassis' willingness and ability to destroy a person's credibility with other players was enough to keep any ambitious associate in line. The willingness and ability of others to do the same to him was the basis of Onassis' own honor. Such men are always practical.

Obviously, there are as many variations of this system as there are people, and there are some individuals more skilled in bartering than others. The game can be extremely subtle and very complex, but bartering, with each person or group negotiating for his best price, is the heart of male social interaction. This is the basis of commerce, salaries, allied defense, and—until recently—marriage. Throughout history, the alternative has been exploitation, which has often led to revolution and war.

Let's look at a typical barter situation. Bill is ready to leave work on Friday for a weekend at the beach when a senior executive stops him in the hall. It seems a report for Monday's important meeting was inadequately researched, and Bill is the very best researcher to prepare a better paper in such a short time. Would Bill mind very much giving up his weekend for the cause?

Bill, if he is deft, may respond, "I've been looking for you, too, George. There is a convention in Hawaii next month I'd like to attend at the company's expense. This convention will benefit the organization since I'll learn some of the newest technical aspects of my job from the leaders in the field." (Bill knows, of course, he will also be in a fine position to meet executives from other companies for future employment should the need arise. He takes good care of himself.)

The barter is on—one weekend for one convention. Neither man at any time mentions who is getting paid to do what job, who is the hardest working employee, who never gets to go to conventions, who is paid to prepare reports, etc.

But, if the senior executive says with a straight face, "I'm sorry, there's no money in the budget for conventions, " Bill responds with the same straight face. "I'm sorry, too, I've rented a house at the beach this weekend," he answers.

Not only do these gentlemen understand the unspoken signals of this game; they also identify each other as poker players, bear fighters, or "good" sports, depending upon the circumstances. Mr. Executive may lose this round; but in the process he will recognize Bill's political acumen and mentally move him onto a faster track in the company.

Of course, it doesn't work exactly this way. More often than not, the executive will counter with a lesser offer. No trip to Hawaii on this one, but how about attendance at the next regional meeting where you will get to meet the big shots in the company? It's like buying a Persian rug, there are no hard-and-fast price tags. What is mutually agreed upon is the barter with each player responsible for meeting his own needs.

It is usual, of course, that Bill, standing at the elevator on Friday afternoon, will not have a particular convention in mind for a passing senior executive with a favor to ask. More likely, Bill will say in effect, "I'll be happy to stay in this weekend, George, because I know who to come to when I need something. *You owe me one.*"

Such words are standard political jargon in this country. To nonplayers, however, "I owe you," is akin to "Thanks, " or "I'll do you a favor sometime *if* it's convenient." To men and women in power those words represent a political contract of the first magnitude—with heavy consequences a la Aristotle Onassis' warning for those who renege on their political obligations. Gathering and relinquishing chips, cashing in, and paying back are realities of men's play. The cost for not playing is exclusion from the "good old boys" network—for women and men alike.

In the opening scene of the movie "The Godfather" Marlon Brando greets an undertaker who has come to him with a grievance. The Sicilian's daughter was raped by two men who had subsequently been given light jail sentences for the offense—inadequate retribution by Italian standards. The father wanted more. The two men negotiated a deal—the rapists would be violently beaten.

The Godfather was delighted to meet the request; after all, he was there to do his people favors. Just remember, he told the undertaker, someday he may ask for a favor in return. And later, when the Godfather's son, Sonny, was killed—the call was made: prepare the body for the funeral so Sonny's mother would not see the brutality of his death. In this case, two beatings were worth one careful embalming. Generally speaking, women are excluded from these games for a variety of reasons. For one thing, we don't understand or recognize them. Even as we leave home and hearth to play on men's turf, we bring with us our own politics which is extraordinarily effective in the one-to-one interactions of home, family, and community—but inappropriate elsewhere. Generally men don't realize we don't know their game. They assume our rather bizarre actions are indicative of incompetence or, as one man said, "viciousness" rather than ignorance of the sport.

Some of us play the bartering game surreptitiously, since our mothers told us it wasn't nice to expect anything in return for our good deeds. Thus we work extremely hard at our jobs, doing the very best we can until we obtain the boss's approval. Then we relax, anticipating that with approval comes our reward—a better project, higher status, a raise, a promotion. Inevitably we're frustrated, since such spoils usually go to players who negotiate for them, signaling their political prowess in the process. Indeed, the major contention between men and women in the work force centers around the female perception that bosses should reward and take care of good employees versus the male perception that good employees are ones who demonstrate the ability to take care of themselves.

CONFLICTING VALUE SYSTEMS

Another barrier for women in the bartering game is the female tendency to impose personal values on situations. It is understandable because just as men learned to disregard personal values in social interaction with one another, women developed and maintained personal power at home by *imposing* their values on others. Such behavior is unacceptable to the white male establishment, because in its extreme it leads to war. (And war is strategically useful only if it enables the players to reach their goals.)

It has been said a man's beliefs cannot be changed. They are made up of the stuff of history, culture,

family, and upbringing. Yet when people shift from
the sacred to the the pragmatic, from principles to
practices, an element of flexibility is injected. In the
interests of negotiation, men ignore individual value
systems.

Value systems are the problem for women in the
"good old boys" network. If Joe owes Robert a favor,
and each has a unique and different value system,
whose values prevail when Joe is asked to pay off?
Most women believe their own values should
predominate. But for savvy men, this is the ultimate
sin. The undertaker doesn't have the opportunity to
determine how he will pay back the Godfather. In a
political debt, Robert determines the payoff. Joe will
impose his own values on the barter at the great cost of
proving his unreliability in future bear hunts.

We learned this graphically several years ago when
conducting a series of training programs with two
other women who had solid theoretical managerial
knowledge, but very little political acumen. We had
arranged to work through a small female-run
consulting firm which was unable to pay for the work
done. Thus, while we were spending our savings to
honor contracts we had negotiated, the consulting firm
was paid for our work and we were not. Within several
months, we found ourselves without income or
savings, but legally tied to contractual work which
eliminated the possibility of obtaining employment
elsewhere—a position known as being between a rock
and a hard place.

Our major resource was to call in our chips with the
other two trainers; if the four of us refused to do
further training under any contract, the consulting
firm, in order to receive any more money, would be

forced to pay what was owed. Not surprisingly, both women invoked their own values in the situation and decided the disappointment of the students looking forward to the training which their organizations had contracted, was more important than our ability to pay our bills. One of us almost went on welfare as a result.

It was then we decided we could no longer afford to simply talk about power; we had to develop and maintain it. Since then, like most of the savvy men we know, we simply refuse to play with women—or men—who operate solely from their own values.

The world of bear fighters is a very dangerous place, and what protection is available comes at a price. It is simply impossible for a business pioneer to depend upon a neighbor to shoot an attacking bear, if the neighbor is going to determine during the crisis she doesn't ever, on principle, hurt an animal representative of an endangered species.

An example of male politics is related by Liz Smith, the gossip columnist. Some years ago Billy Rose decided to buy a particular building in Chicago for sentimental reasons. Joe Kennedy had bid for the same structure, at a price beyond Billy Rose's means. Billy asked Joe to buy another building so he could fulfill a childhood fantasy. Joe was happy to comply. Many years later, Joe's son, Jack, was the Democratic candidate for president at a time when Billy was heavily involved in Republican fundraising. Joe, calling in his chip, reminded Billy of the old favor and asked the showman to stop working against his son. Billy did. Ari Onassis would have understood.

Obviously, the obligation to pay political debts creates new perspectives. Bright men are very wary from whom they ask favors. They don't borrow money from the Mafia unless they are willing to meet the terms. And they don't ask for a job from someone who may ask them to do something unacceptable in return.

When men don't want to enter into a barter, for whatever reason, they are rarely direct about it. That kind of disclosure is usually dangerous. Instead, they invoke rules or finances. They reply, "I'd love to help you, but this company has a firm policy about the necessity for an advanced degree in that job;" or "Of course you deserve to attend the conference, isn't it too bad we had to cut that item out of the budget this year?"

Disclosure, frankness, and revelation are not useful tactics in any male sport for they tend to be obstructive and ineffective. For this reason many females consider businessmen and politicians devious and deceitful. But we have little experience with quarterback sneaks and closely held cards. Women promote "honesty," by which we mean the right to say whatever we feel about someone without having to pay the consequence. Whenever a woman says she wants to be honest these days, as often as not she is about to insult someone.

The Japanese language contains words used only by males and others used only by females. If the same were true of English, "bluff" would be a masculine verb. It has no apparent relationship to female behavior at all, for women are said to "lie" or "deceive" instead.

There is a "party line" for almost every business, political, and social interaction. The reason for getting married, for example, is "love." Pregnancy by an unknown father, romantic rebound, the lure of money, and revenge are also popular motives. But to reveal such motivations would bring unfortunate and predictable consequences. Similarly, corporate promotions are always said to be on the basis of "competence"—even though blackmail, sex, and luck are just as likely to be the impetus.

We women encourage this kind of communication, by which men willingly accommodate us. They tell us tokens exist in other organizations, not our own.

When the Equal Employment Opportunity Act was passed in 1963, outlawing the refusal to hire or promote people on the basis of sex, religion, race, and age, Congress simply made it unsafe for an employer to use any reason against a prospect except two: "you don't have the right credentials," or "you are unqualified"—whatever that means. The result is we are no longer told the real reason we get or lose a job.

Thus competent men learn early to conceal their motives, their goals, and their strategies, trading instead, in a "safe" doctrine with those they don't trust. There is sound reason for this: no one is totally powerless, and the readily available and most used power tool of the weak is obstruction of the goals of the strong. The killing of Anwar Sadat is an example of obstructive behavior at its worst. That murder did not enable the assassins to achieve any of their social programs. In fact, it made it less likely such programs would be adopted. It did, however, keep Sadat from achieving his aims.

People in the know understand anyone has the power to obstruct them, but they also realize most people will be pacified by an *appearance* of power, a promise, or an "ain't it awful, we're in this together" message. Thus, while the power game is played in broad daylight, available to anyone who knows how to watch it, the verbal communication around it is apt to be misleading and inaccurate.

BREAKING THE COMMUNICATION CODE

Savvy men play in metacommunicative code. While there are no rules underlying this language, it is often restricted by usage to those who are known to be power players. Metacommunication is a far more reliable indicator of the real games of power in any given instance. Metacommunication is the sum total of *all* communication, including words, silence, absence, body language, inflection, skin color, room decor, weather, the availability or unavailability of food, washrooms and other aspects of life.

Because of this metacommunication, the same words spoken by a powerful man have different meaning when uttered by a woman, at least until she has earned her proverbial stripes. Consequently a male player who signifies his knowingness by asking, "What can I do for you?" (usually unspoken is the ending of the sentence: "...in return for which...") is recognized as someone who is creating some chips for a rainy day. He is also understood to be asking, "Do you want to play with me?"

The same phrase from a woman's mouth has a very different connotation. It often signifies the speaker is probably a "do-gooder" seeking approval, really asking for help, or simply offering to do a favor without evoking the power process.

Yet women can access the code. A young woman was offered a very key position in a company in which a male acquaintance had good connections. After she said several times, "You know, if there's anything I can do for you once I'm hired, please let me know," he looked at her in amazement and responded, "You *understand* what you're saying, don't you? You really comprehend the game." His past experiences had led him to discount those words when spoken by a female.

Men do speak in code to us all the time. Any woman over the age of 16 can tell whether or not a verbal invitation to dinner is only that. We respond in code of our own: dinner is fine, but then I've got a headache. The metacommunication completes the subtle, yet incisive, message.

One of the continuing political errors made by NOW was blaming the insurance companies for the defeat of the ERA. The metacommunication was that insurance companies have more power over the future of women than does an organization with 20 years of effort at developing such influence. A manufacturer of women's products, eager to put money into influencing female thinking, had considered investing in NOW, but instead approached a life insurance company because even the feminist leadership admitted his money would buy him more leverage there.

5.
Non-
Confrontation

Power games aren't played with a heavy hand. In chess, for instance, one rarely charges full tilt for the king, but employs elaborate distractions, sacrifices, and contortions. While all games are easy to observe once one learns to recognize and interpret the signals, most political activity is carried out behind closed doors, in code, or otherwise masked. Players find it too risky to publicly discuss the technology of political play. Nevertheless, while we are undergoing "assertiveness training," men are learning about camouflage, subterfuge, poker faces, and plea bargaining.

Women are learning how to confront—nicely, of course, we can't be too aggressive—while men are gaining skills in non-confrontation, a far more effective ploy. Head-on confrontations too often produce even more entrenched positions. When the toes are dug in, eyeballs staring into eyeballs, the end result is usually more strident assertions, rather than compromise. Yet there are results-oriented games that do deliver.

Non-confrontation is a tactic successfully used by politic men. It is, in fact, one of the talents of smart women in traditional roles. Only when women use it, it isn't called non-confrontation, it's called manipulation.

When children need protein, we do not sit them down and discuss nutrition. Children are skilled enough in political warfare, and we don't need to provide them with any more ammunition. Instead, we can ask them if they would like milkshakes and offer to bring them out back where they are playing. Then, by slipping a couple of raw eggs into the blender, we have accomplished our objective without ever raising the issue. Non-confrontation!

All the while the male bear fighters complain loudly women are too manipulative—with the consequence that approval-seeking females join in condemning their so-called manipulating sisters. Thus the menfolk effectively manipulate us with non-confrontational techniques.

LINE VS. STAFF POSITIONS

When Congress passed the Equal Employment Opportunity Act in 1963, virtually every organization in the country, and especially the federal government itself, created thousands upon thousands of staff "nonjobs" in which women and minority males were placed. Of course, the organizations had functioned quite well *without* these positons and would again, but political expediency required adoption of nonoperational spots for nonplayers. As a result, businesses had to increase their budgets and the cost of goods and services to pay for these positions. This is one reason why inflation rampaged during the early 1970s. This particular game is well ensconced today, yet most women don't even realize its existence. (Many black men figured it out and moved quickly into the mainstream.) The vast majority of working women today do not understand this sleight of hand: the difference between line and staff work.

Line people inherently have more power than support personnel just by the nature of their jobs. What they do is *essential* to the organization. In our company, for example, the line personnel are directly involved in the product or in the selling of training and consulting services and products. Everyone else is staff, including the accountant and the attorney. When we train in a university we are line people because the school sells what we produce. When we do the same training for an organization, however, we are staff functionaries because we do not produce what the company sells.

Line people, those in production and sales, have more status, more power, more security, more recognition, and more leverage than staff personnel. A staff position is out of the main flow of production. Also, and inevitably, the line in every organization of size in the U.S. is controlled by the white male establishment. In February of 1984, *Working Women* magazine pointed out 96% of all female managers in the U.S. are in staff positions.

Very often women misinterpret the bias line people always have toward staff employees as sexism, simply because women are invariably bunched up on the wrong side—in staff positions. The policeman on the beat naturally knows the report writer back at the precinct doesn't understand what it's like to risk his life. The air traffic controller in the tower resents the

statistician who compiles data. The salesman of
industrial equipment doesn't take a backseat to the
company attorney. The medic in the field understands
and manipulates the supply sergeant's position.

Of course, when men talk about the increasing
influence of women in their businesses, they inevitably
avoid the reality that virtually all of the women have
been carefully sidelined, or sidestaffed. Everyone gets
to feel "wonderful;" there are visible women, and the
game goes on. (While it is true women are now
entering line positions at bottom rungs in organizations, the worst of them flunk out. And most of the
others are promoted to staff jobs.)

Staff jobs have been around longer than women in
business. Men find staff jobs important for the
organization; but also useful tools in developing and
maintaining their own power. There is less risk
involved in staff work and less visibility. Often young
accountants, for example, will take staff positions with
retailers while they learn the game and hone their
skills. When they feel themselves polished, they will
move into accounting firms as line players. Rarely a
particularly strong staff vice-president will exert more
power and influence than weak line executives. Harold
Geneen is such an example. He was able to leverage his
staff position to move into the catbird seat of power as
the former CEO of ITT.

Another non-confrontational manipulation of
women revolves around "qualifications." When senior
men talk about moving up only qualified people, they
usually mean those who are politically ept. Women
hear this as "technically competent." Most female
employees can't figure out how the company officials
can keep talking about the need for qualified people at

the top when the keep moving up people who are technically unproductive.

Not all non-confrontations are primed against women. Common non-confrontational strategies exist throughout business, politics, and industry, and are utilized with vehemence. Women often simply have a more difficult time understanding them and tend to personalize such tactics when they are uncovered. Often, when a businesswoman decries a certain policy or action as "unfair," it is because she has found herself disadvantaged by a non-confrontational manipulation. However, the charge is seldom voiced when she benefits from such strategies.

USING RULES AND MONEY

The Office of Personnel Management (OPM), formerly the Civil Service Commission, creates regulations for government employees apparently based on the premise that power development is unethical and not nice. Some of the restrictions it imposes upon government executives border on fantasy. The requirement, for example, to hire and promote people only on the basis of their professional or technical expertise is like going bear hunting with a switch. As any manager can tell you, good leadership requires followers who have demonstrated their loyalty, political skill, and toughness. None of that is conveyed on a resume.

Thus, in and out of the government, the process of "wiring jobs" has risen to an art form. Basically, a manager will identify someone he wants on his team, then advertise a position which just happens to require skills only the aforementioned person exhibits on his biographical data.

When a promotion panel is required, it is fairly simple to stack it with friendly faces or to befuddle them with buzzwords. A high ranking government executive confessed his greatest achievement in thirty years was to amass his team of 50 people in spite of OPM regulations.

Since it is difficult to fire people in the government, officials rely heavily on two non-confrontational tools—reorganization and budget. Through both, power can be shifted, defiant employees neutralized, and business centralized in the hands of the powerful few—a situation which leads to the charge that many government employees are doing little of value.

Reorganizations are common practice in federal offices. Sometimes elaborate shifts are engineered just to get rid of two or three people who are bottlenecking the mission. Sometimes, reorganizations are used to create dead-end routes for nonplayers and open creative pathways for more valued team members. It is common to give some employees busy work and to send their work through channels that constrain and restrict their activities. Other employees either have bosses who restrict nothing or know through codes and connections they can safely disregard the regulations hampering their coworkers.

Budget is also a handy variable. "I'm sorry, there's no money in the budget," is often used to say, "I don't owe you anything and I don't want you doing what you want to do." Women often find themselves stymied by budgets which somehow always expand when men are involved. We've learned, even when we do our nationwide seminars strictly for women, to sell men on the program rather than their female peers. Why?

Because women very often find "there's no money in the budget," while smart males know how to shake the financial tree.

TACTICS FOR CRISIS SOLVING

National politics also provide excellent non-confrontational opportunities. Americans, sorry to say, do not value people who *prevent* problems, only those who solve them. Dwight Eisenhower has been called a "do-nothing" president because there were few crises during his administration—no riots, no wars, no inflation, no recession, and no grasshopper plague. This problem has not been lost on his successors who, thanks to television and the proliferation of instant media, are often dependent upon the whims of a fickle public for program support and political longevity.

Since Eisenhower's day, almost every president has served his first two years in office with some tranquility—only to face charges of inactivity and indecisiveness as a result. Public popularity of the incumbent inevitably plummets after he has spent some time in office. Magically, a crisis arises—the Malaguez incident with President Ford—in which the President can demonstrate his courage, control, and effectiveness. And magically, again his popularity rises. Margaret Thatcher had her Falkland Islands to prove her mettle when the British Empire needed to restore its pride. John Kennedy showed his macho toughness and regained national respect by following the disastrous Bay of Pigs incident with the more admired "missle crisis."

About a year into his first term, Ronald Reagan was stung by public polls belittling his foreign relations skills. Several months later, two Iraqi fighter pilots were caught invading American air space. These "incidents" were not caused by the administration in charge (no one has that kind of power); but they were certainly exploited by them in the press. Reagan's reputation as a "strong" president increased drastically after he ordered the planes shot down.

Business people, too, create crises in order to achieve a goal. One of our clients is the chief nurse at a hospital. She faced a serious problem. The hospital administrator was saving money by cutting the personnel budget and eliminating orderlies and nursing aides. This decision forced the R.N.s to work extra hours, take on extra duties, and assume extra responsibilities. Morale plummeted. Many of the nurses quit. Replacements were difficult to find and more difficult to hire. The situation was such that life-threatening mistakes were being made in the preparation of medicines for the patients.

Our client, Roberta, spoke to the administrator several times to no avail. She then proposed the nurses strike until conditions improved. The women refused, concerned for the patients already in the hospital. In desperation, Roberta came to Operational Politics, Inc. for advice. We devised a plan. Henceforth, all patients were to be fed one to two hours late, after all medications and nursing routines had been attended to. Only those patients who were in intensive care or fed intravenously were exempted from our ploy.

There is nothing so sacred to a hospital patient on the mend as mealtime. Pandemonium greeted the hospital administrator the day after this plan took effect. Complaints proliferated from every floor, every ward, and every wing. Doctors yelled, kitchen attendants balked, and families fumed. The administrator, feeling this wrath, confronted Roberta. "What the hell are you doing?" he demanded. "Why," she answered sweetly, "I've instructed my nurses to attend to medical business first and to take care of other duties if and when they find the time. You wouldn't want it any other way, would you?" As you might expect, the budget was rapidly increased to allow for nursing aides.

Richard Buskirk, in his *Handbook of Management Techniques*, cites this example: A group of young architects learned whenever someone else had to review their work, invariably their painstakingly created designs were changed. The senior architects felt they weren't doing their jobs if they let junior plans go through untouched. Hence, the youngsters always included an extraneous window in the designs for their superiors to "discover" and eliminate. They knew once the window was altered, the rest of the plan was acceptable. The older men felt they had maintained control.

We counseled a publishing client to use a variation of this tactic while he was trying to raise money for a political magazine. He was intellectually brilliant, particularly in language and communication. His proposals were veritable works of poetry. That was the problem. He was so talented he intimidated everyone who read his plans. Moneylenders who had made fortunes through venture capital risks were put off because they felt working with him would constantly remind them of their own comparative stupidity. More than eight financiers turned him down—while publicly extolling his brilliance to their cohorts.

We suggested he purposely put a glaring mistake right in the middle of his work so the next prospective investor, while still impressed with the man's intelligence, would be able to say to himself, "This guy isn't so great after all, I can handle him."

Many women believe such tactics are unfair and unethical because they, themselves, have no recourse against non-confrontation. Power players believe, however, people are in charge of their own lives and can choose to participate or not, according to the benefit they may or may not receive. Our kids can always refuse the milkshakes, American voters can begin to value presidents who prevent problems, and hospital administrators can cooperate more closely with nursing supervisors.

Most non-confrontational tactics are mutually beneficial, because otherwise negative consequences can result. Good manners are an example of arbitrary behavior that allows everyone to protect their egos while doing business with enemies or opponents. In Japan, because there are so many people on so little land, politeness is politically essential, for behind its facade is often the only privacy an individual enjoys. In that country especially, people ignore etiquette at great personal expense to themselves.

Many people are horrified by feminist leaders' overuse of insult and defamation as a tactical procedure. Men, of course, can resort to the same behavior—but the difference was put into perspective for Pauline by a male power player with whom she was having lunch. He was late, he apologized, because the damn women in his office had spent the last month backbiting one another to the point it had gotten out of hand, and he'd had to step in.

Feeling defensive for women, Pauline countered "damn men" regularly stab each other in the back.

Well yes, he said, men do, but they *do it in order to gain something*. Men attack each other in order to get each other's jobs, diminish one another's influence, discredit each other's programs, and so on. Women belittle other women, *just to do it*. Politeness, etiquette, diplomacy, tact, and like skills are ignored at great personal expense. The payoff for maintaining them may not be a seat at the poker table, but it will at least provide an invitation to the room to watch and learn.

6.
Quid
Pro Quo

Good bear fighters do not take care of each other. They do have compassion and they demonstrate it frequently. They take care of injured bear fighters, the sick, the weak, the young, and the elderly. They don't take care of each other, they can't. It is insulting for a healthy and masterful fighter to treat another as if he were weak and unskilled. In fact, powerful men do this to one another only as a ploy to sap the confidence of an adversary. Usually power is a shared process, an exchange between men of similar rank and abilities.

NEGOTIATION IS BORN

Thus negotiation was developed. It provides an alternative to fist fighting, mugging, head-bashing, and armed conflict. All bartering is negotiation without a price tag. While in reality there are no price tags, the female need for security often demands one. We want to know when we do someone a favor (finish up a project over the weekend), he owes us commensurate time off, a ticket to the convention, or a three percent salary increase. (More often, we are paid with verbal approval, promises, and feelings. This is what we communicate we want, and what we often accept.)

Not all negotiations are verbal and formal. Even those that are, involve a variety of unspoken communication. But at its basic state, negotiation is simply two or more people making independent decisions to agree to a process or goal.

Ralph agrees to take Nancy to the store in return for which she agrees to go—or to cook dinner—or to sleep with him—or to spend the rest of her life in abject servitude.

Obviously, the circumstances matter. The store may be 10 miles away. Ralph may have the only car in town. The store may be giving a fur coat to the first 10 women who can get there. Ralph may have made a bet with his pals Nancy would go out with him. Circumstances determine motivation; motivation provides a basis for leverage. Leverage is never equal. But the decision is made independently by the two people involved.

Frank, who is the boss, hires Jim. Jim agrees to do A, B, and C in return for D. Then the boss hires Paul, who agrees to do the same amount of work in return for much more than just D. Jim, the first employee, is angry, but he doesn't want to lose his job, so he contacts a third party, Bill, who agrees to negotiate his job with the boss. Bill gets Jim a better deal than Paul's. Now Paul is angry. He has a college degree and Jim doesn't, plus he has more experience than Jim. He also knows more influential people. Paul uses this leverage to negotiate with a friend in the Senate to introduce a law restricting jobs like his to people with college degrees.

The boss gets concerned. This could cost him a lot of money and lose him good, non-degreed employees. He talks with an influential friend, Greg, who negotiates with the Senator. Bill wants in on the negotiation to represent Jim's interests. Greg and Bill end up joining forces, even though at other times they are at opposite poles.

This is how unions, lobbies, legislation, and contracts are formed. Other issues come into play as leverage changes. Bill, for example, may have agreed to represent other Jims in other companies who may be college graduates. They would prefer he negotiate the "other side of the table" and get the legislation passed. He is now in a no-win situation because no matter what he does, someone will feel he has not kept his agreement to get the best deal for his people.

Negotiation is clearly not just a man's game for we women negotiate all the time. It's just that once again successful men do it with different insights, goals, and consequences.

UNDERSTANDING GENDER CONTRASTS

The contrast was demonstrated to us clearly by a situation which effected two different clients. Delores had recently left her job to become a management consultant. Her first order of business was to write a proposal for a government contract. She was smart enough to realize her professional skills were not sufficient—she needed to pay attention to the politics. So she contacted Jack, a consultant of long and successful standing, to get some critical information. She queried him about where to send the proposal,

whose names should be invoked in the cover letter, and
what references should be cited.

She offered no money, and Jack asked for none. He
gave her the information she requested. It proved to be
instrumental, along with her proposal, in garnering
the contract. At this point, Delores recognized she
owed Jack something, so she contacted him and asked,
"What do you want?" "50 percent," He answered.

Delores was furious. She slammed down the phone
feeling justified in offering him nothing. After all, *she*
had spent three months putting together the proposal
while he had given her 10 minutes of advice.

This incident illustrates perfectly the difference
between male and female negotiation. Delores first
called Jack and asked for help, without a corresponding
recognition of obligation. Jack understandably
perceived her as charity. This was not barter, but one-
sided assistance, a male protecting a weaker female. He
was happy to oblige.

Delores' nurturing instincts were aroused when she
received the contract. In fairness she wanted to take
care of Jack. She had a preconceived, if subconscious,
price tag in mind before she called him. Unwittingly,
she set herself up when she asked what Jack wanted.
For Delores, the statement was merely a polite
beginning—a technique to signal *her* kind of
negotiation.

But for Jack, it was the overture to the kind of
bartering he had mastered years before. He fully
expected Delores to respond, "You're crazy. I did most
of the work. You gave me 10 minutes. That's worth
five percent."

To which he would have said, "My 10 minutes got
you the contract. Forty percent." Her ball: "My

contacts were just as good as yours; you just told me what to do with them. Ten percent." His: "How about 20 percent and an introduction to the head man at the agency?" To this Delores might have countered, "15 percent and lunch for the three of us." At some point they would have found mutual agreement.

Jack did not recognize Delores' game as different from his own because she invoked his terminology. Had he thought about it, he would have known Delores was communicating something else because of her charity request months before.

Delores' need for protection was violated when Jack said, "50 percent." She took that as law, particularly since the words came from a male, who presumably created and enforced "the rules." She invoked process and values and exclusion. Specifically, she disapproved of his tactics and unilaterally excluded him from this negotiation and any further business.

Jack still doesn't know what happened. His experience led him to believe even bad negotiators negotiate as long as the goal—securing the contract—is unquestioned. He wouldn't presume to judge Delores' motives or her offers; he had only to accept or reject with a counteroffer. The deal is made when both parties, for whatever reasons, independently decide to agree to the terms. How else do civilized people operate, he wonders?

PROTECTION FROM OUR WEAKNESS

Many of us mistake unfairness and discrimination for the lack of our own ability to negotiate. One of our former OPI clients held a Ph.D. in Entomology from a Midwestern university. Her biggest dream, while in graduate school, was to work in Washington, DC at the Smithsonian Institute. Her defined objective was to be associated with that esteemed organization. She achieved her goal when she was offered a job as a word processor in a Smithsonian laboratory for $15,000 a year.

Several months later, while she was toiling happily at the keyboard, she noticed a former male classmate walking down the hall. She was outraged and incensed to discover he held a position as a junior entomologist at almost double her salary.

While her anger was focused toward management who had "exploited" her, it was misdirected. Her lack of negotiating ability, her insecurity, and her low aspirations (only to be associated with the Smithsonian rather than actually contribute to it) resulted in her accepting the word processing job.

It eventually became clear this woman was angry at having been offered the word processing job to begin with, but that was a veiled demand for protection from any risk taking. She pointed out her male colleague had not been offered so demeaning a position. The recruiter knew better. If he had offered a young male Ph.D. a typing job, the candidate would have laughed, yelled, walked, or counteroffered; he wouldn't have agreed. Women do agree, and in so doing we encourage the next recruiter to offer the next woman the same thing. "There's no harm in asking," he thinks. "She can always refuse."

The problem is we believe we have no leverage; nothing to offer in return. In a sense this is true. We often don't recognize our own worth, don't gather "chips" before the negotiation, and don't know how to play the leverage we do possess. We don't realize power—like a boomerang—has to be thrown out before it comes back.

Instead we demand protection: laws regulating pay, recruitment, and employment. By so doing, we create tokenism, for the men know whatever that is, it isn't poker. It isn't equality. The person who can't negotiate for herself, who can't take care of herself during initial dickering between herself and the company that employs her, has signaled to all she cannot take care of herself in any ensuing bear fight. Consequently she doesn't qualify for the hunt.

Unions are formed to protect men with similar difficulties; but unions protect the weak. Their members have no place among the leadership. Management must take care of itself, It has no unions. (Unions are also only as effective as *their* management; savvy leaders are essential everywhere.)

Male power players know their bottom lines, the minimums they will accept in any barter. They see no need to disclose these, however, for by bluffing they may increase their benefits. They also recognize they are not in charge of setting minimums for anyone else. They presume the right to offer anything they want in a negotiation. They also presume the right of their adversaries to refuse and counteroffer.

Forceful men rarely allow others to negotiate for them, because they would lose advantage, although they commonly ask others to represent them at the negotiating table. Representatives can ascertain the culture, environment, and weaknesses of the adversaries, even though they do not themselves make decisions. That privilege is reserved for the leadership.

MAKING LEVERAGE A FRIEND

The skill and resilience of accomplished male bear fighters allows them to benefit from almost any circumstance that arises. Successful negotiators are always trying to increase their leverage; the more laws on the books, the more influence attorneys and government regulators possess. Civil laws are particularly useful because they use money as the currency of power rather than incarceration, which is becoming too expensive a system to maintain.

Children understand this concept well. Little Johnny draws a line and decides, unilaterally, Paul cannot cross it. The risk is Paul may refuse to agree, cross it anyway, and expose Johnny's lack of power. Johnny will then have to impose his authority physically—or admit he is powerless. But if Paul agrees Johnny's line is inviolate and in the way of where he wants to go, Johnny has created some leverage for himself. He can remove his line in return for whatever bargain Paul makes.

Modern legislative solutions rarely cure problems; they do create leverage. The problems are resolved in direct proportion to the skills of the bear fighters in using influence. A cynicism which arose during Lyndon Johnson's presidency was that there is money to be made in poverty. Many people leveraged his legislative ideals into personal or organizational benefit for themselves. Some of the poor were helped; some were not. Some were also said to be helped who were not. Others were helped and said to be still at the same level of need, for leverage is created by changing or maintaining political *perceptions* among the public.

Leverage is also formed by favors, in the manner we discussed earlier. Politically proficient men try to obligate others to them, so in times of adversity they can call upon an army of loyal lieutenants and foot soldiers. They also recognize the need to be occasionally obligated themselves, to demonstrate their equal willingness to fight others' bears. Although there is no price tag, there is a sort of quid pro quo in operation.

Little Paul, however punier he is, can gain equal advantage when he challenges Johnny's line—if he does so backed by four of his friends. Of course he has to give something for their protection. It is not automatic.

Women used to barter sex and family for protection, and sometimes still do, although too many of us think we can substitute professional and technical skills instead. Unfortunately, such skills usually buy only money.

The game gets considerably complicated when all the hidden agendas are included. Jinx regularly does business with a shrewd bear fighter who has typical male ego needs around women. He likes her because she is loyal and can deliver the goods. She also gives him feisty repartee, a competitive game between men and women that is sometimes called "good, clean fun."

On one occasion, she was the sole female in an informal meeting with this man's subordinates when in he walked. Delighted to see her, he immediately shot a barb in her direction, prepared for the usual return thrust. But the game was suddenly different. To beat him here was to humiliate him in front of his male team. Dire consequences would surely have surfaced during the next contract negotiation. So instead of quipping a fast come back, she smiled demurely and said, "I'm no match for your wit, Bob. I'm just a lady tryin' to raise my children. I know better than to take you on." Thus his ego—and our contract—was saved.

Losing the battle to win the war is essentially an advanced male technique. Modern women don't usually perceive retreats as strategy, but as failure. Unfortunately many otherwise good men also have problems here. As one gentleman admitted, "Too many men are ruled by their egos and gonads." The exalted male ego can turn many a good bear fighter into the Shah of Iran, unaware of the strength of his opposition until it is too late. Nevertheless, there is often power in losing.

WHEN VALUES GET IN THE WAY

Occasionally, where there is no acceptable alternative barter, men have to negotiate around other's values. (The conflict between the Northern Irish Catholics and Protestants comes to mind.) In such instances, ingrained hatred and a history of past complaints make bartering difficult. When values are involved, particularly when men have already turned to violence, negotiations become extremely sensitive and complex.

One strategy often employed in such situations is to pick an issue around which there is no essential disagreement and use it for practice. Both parties learn how to negotiate with one another until there is a history of some accord on which to build a continuing relationship. This is exactly what happened in the Paris Peace Talks over the Vietnam War. The first 18 months were spent negotiating about the shape of the table. In the process each team took the others' measure. They determined styles, ego needs, weaknesses, leverage, hidden agendas, and the level of seriousness—all without compromising the real issue at hand. Negotiating strategy was then developed to meet the precise circumstances.

This tactic is usually used with terrorists or others who have taken hostages. The initial negotiations focus on such issues as food and room temperature until the government arbitrators can determine the exact situation they are dealing with. It has been noted a female terrorist will typically refuse to negotiate at all. She is usually taking orders from a man, and once he has made a decision, ("If our people aren't released by 5 P.M., shoot one of the hostages,") she will nearly always do it regardless. In such cases, the police try to find the man instructing her and deal with him directly.

Because the participants change their targets, negotiations change as the stakes get higher. In low stakes games, it is easy to concentrate on what one might gain. As the stakes increase, however, many individuals—and organizations—begin to concentrate instead on what they can lose. Savvy players know to increase the risk against low power opponents. And once more, women are unprepared by training and experience to operate beyond the penny ante game. It is often enough, during an employment negotiation where a woman is trying to gain a raise, to suggest her job is being eliminated. It is extremely difficult for the majority of us to keep focused on our original goal and call the bluff.

We also are not prepared to walk away. Smart men will often forfeit a goal rather than give in to an unsuitable compromise. Early union men went without work rather than accept jobs paying low wages. Black leaders in the deep South during the early 1960s initiated boycotts and protests rather than ride in the back of the bus. The budding male entomologist would have given up the Smithsonian rather than type.

Walking away from the table doesn't necessarily mean the negotiation is over; it's just changed. Sometimes it means the next negotiation is about getting back to the table; sometimes it is a tactic for buying time; sometimes an emotional release; and sometimes "no deal."

THE PERSEVERANCE EDGE

No negotiation is ever over until the parties agree to spend their energies elsewhere. Route 66, outside of Washington, DC in suburban Virginia, is a monument to negotiating tenacity. For as long as Jinx can remember, that road had been proposed and turned down by a variety of federal and state legislatures and regulatory agencies. Major opposition was concentrated in the communities that would be disrupted by a highway serving mainly commuters. Yet, the highway proposal kept coming back year after year. Route 66 is now a reality.

On the other side of the city is another road, Interstate Highway 95, from New York City and points north to Florida. It was planned to go through Maryland suburbs to connect with Virginia. But the fate of this thoroughfare was very different. Instead of finishing it as required by the Federal Highway Administration to complete the interstate system, another barter was substituted. Maryland officials simply named an existing artery Interstate Highway 95!

Negotiating tenacity is highly valued in corporate salespeople who understand today's "no" actually means "maybe," and could be tomorrow's "yes." Never say never to the skilled—and hungry—bear fighter. It's not surprising so many men believe a female "no" to be like any other. Our insistence that our every "no"—sexual or otherwise—always means "no," may result in our being disqualified by men from negotiating anything on their terms. If they come to see us as rigid in every instance, a new double standard may ensue. We'll be using two different currencies: rules for us and negotiations for them. In some places, this is already happening.

7.
Currencies

What do the power brokers barter? Anything and everything! This is a game with high risk and great consequence. Most good players offer to barter what someone else needs, less astute people will offer what they have most of. The real pros will barter what *others need most* whether or not they have it to begin with.

FINANCIAL BARTERS

A major currency in America is money...or things money can buy. A salary is simply a payoff of a barter. A person agrees to do a job in return for which he or she receives certain financial benefits. The deal is set the day the employee starts work. Most promotions and raises come from new negotiations. Higher job responsibilities go to people who demonstrate they can handle them and who negotiate for them. Promotions are rarely rewards for past work well done.

There are many other kinds of financial barters. Goods and services in this society are usually traded for money. People barter in department stores or at yard sales. They hire hair dressers or babysitters, real estate agents or cab drivers. Money is exchanged directly or indirectly, as in automobile trade-ins. And while goods and services are a popular bartering currency, they are dangerous because there is little difference between prostitution, bribery, or legitimate fees. Two of these actions are punishable in court, but who can always differentiate between what is legal and what is not?

One of the easiest things in the world is to set someone up to look as if he or she has done something illegal. Damning circumstantial evidence can be arranged. For example, it is a simple matter to open a bank account in the name of anyone without his or her knowledge, and make regular large deposits. Then at some later date it can be arranged for a known junkie to "admit" the person in question was involved regularly in drug deals. Some stashed paraphenalia, a few "witnesses" and who can tell? The lines between kickbacks, gifts, lotteries, inheritances, and blackmail are precariously slim—what looks like an innocent gift when viewed from one perspective may be seen as a bribe from another.

For this reason power brokers use many other currencies. Things money can buy enjoy greater usage. Football game tickets, country club memberships, lunches, special brand liquors, Cuban cigars, all are common barter items. In certain circles cocaine and marijuana prevail. Especially popular are business Christmas presents. They're hard gifts to refuse and are tax deductible.

GAINING ACCESS TO POWER PLAYERS

In Denver, Colorado, one of the great power brokers, Marvin Davis, owner of Twentieth Century Fox, hosts an annual fund-raising charity ball for the Juvenile Diabetes Foundation. Those who pay upwards of $200 per couple to attend buy more than good dance music. The unintiated often think people spend money just to be seen at posh functions. But proficient players know better. For their tax-deductible contributions, they trade five or six hours of access to Mr. Davis and other superstars of the business and entertainment worlds. Those with the money and moxie to buy a whole table not only barter access for themselves but also for those they invite to join them. The invitees, of course, are beholden to their host for the privilege.

Trips to foreign lands, ocean cruises, hunting expeditions, and the like are big-time bartering tools. For less affluent comers there are seats at the ballet, entrance to exclusive country clubs, or a basket of choice apples.

One day when Jinx was giving a speech in Columbus, Ohio, she was met at the airport by a chauffeur and limousine, hired by the garden club members she was addressing. As she thanked them for the luxurious ride, they blushed it was nothing; they had only wanted her to be comfortable. By the way, would she do them a favor when she returned home to Washington, DC? There was a bill of interest to them pending in Congress; would she mind visiting their state representative to explain how these women felt about this particular legislation? Those homemakers bartered a limousine ride for her lobbbying activity.

Most powerful men won't sell out for a ride in a
fancy car. More likely they'd have turned down the
invitation on the pretext they already had transpor-
tation and thank you very much. Nevertheless, that
kind of chutzpah from a group of homemakers would
have impressed Onassis himself.

Business lunchs are probably the most common
barters because they are relatively quick, cheap, and
painless ways to take one another's measure. Who pays
is very political; but many neophytes insist on always
grabbing the bill—to their detriment. The person who
never pays loses the advantage of having others in his
debt. To alway pick up the tab, however, is just as
limiting.

TAPPING THE INFORMATION HOT LINE

Material things are probably the cheapest of all
bartering tools. Information is by far more valuable.
Knowledge certainly is power, and there are many
kinds of knowledge. A person who can fly an airplane
has an automatic chip with someone who wants a ride.

Other kinds of knowledge may be worth more.
Particularly valuable is the who-is-sleeping-with-
whom information often denied as office gossip.
Executives know managerial effectiveness often
depends upon knowing who is promiscuous, who is
lazy, who is reliable, who is spreading rumors. George
may need to know Sally is pregnant, not because he
cares about her personal life, but because he is about to
recommend she attend systems analysis school—a
program costing his company over $10,000—only to
have her quit her job three weeks after the school ends.
He needs to know Harry drinks, not because George

hates alcohol, but because George's predecessor left Harry in charge while away on business and if George does the same thing, Harry and the office will go to pieces.

That kind of information is difficult for managers to come by, given the silent conspiracy of people at the bottom against those at the top. Low ranking people with access to such gossip can use it to build their own personal power bases, if they are not busy throwing it away at the lunch table to all who will listen.

As restrictions are placed on access to one another, information becomes more valuable. In militaristic systems which preclude going above a superior's head to his superior, information received at the top requires greater risk and can be used to negotiate a higher premium. Thus, restrictive lines of communication simply foster better data bartering, which is one reason why such systems exist.

Solid information about opposing teams, competitors, armies, even countries is most valued of all data. It therefore carries the highest risks and rewards, even to being extolled as a hero or condemned as a traitor, depending on what is traded to whom for what purpose and to what effect the information is used.

USING STATUS SYMBOLS

Another useful bartering tool is status. Nonplayers often mistake status as a reward given to them for competent work. They think the purpose of the large office is to impress others with their importance or to enable themselves to revel in earned luxury. Politic men and women know better.

Many organizations create status symbols in order

to provide their people with things to barter. The value of the large office is for Henry to be able to say to his subordinate: "You have an important negotiation today? Use my place;" or "Take my car;" or "I'll have my secretary do it for you;" or "I'm on an expense account; let me pay for dinner."

Every organization has its own variety of status symbols, material and nonmaterial. Windows, carpeting, parking spots, and the like are fairly common in America. Nonmaterial status is usually more important. Privacy is a popular bartering mechanism—single person offices, private bath-rooms, and dining salons. So is accessibility—private phone lines, meeting invitations, exclusive club membership. Accountability is also bartered; status is conferred on those who do not have to punch time clocks, keep lunch hours, arrive or stay at the office according to an arbitrary deadline, attend certain meetings, use expense accounts, etc. Time is a barterable item. There are those who arrive early and stay late; those who arrive late and leave early; those who get paid by the hour and those who are compensated by the job.

Some status items are subtle. John calls Bill by his first name and Bill calls John, Mr. Bates. The game is incurred when the boss says, "Come on, Bill, call me John." This is apt to be code for "Bill, you can play on my team;" or it may mean, "Bill, I'm giving you access to us guys upstairs; just remember you owe me for this;" or "Bill, I recognize the favors you've done for me and I'm paying you off with recognition among the superplayers that you are a good player." (It can also mean, "Bill, you make me uncomfortable calling me Mr. Bates;" or "I wish everyone would call me by my first name;" or just "Call me John.")

The best status symbols are covert. A power player of the first magnitude, who was publisher of a major magazine, lived in a very exclusive, high-powered community outside New York City. During the late 1960s, when easy dollars were made in the stock market, outsiders—abounding with new money and little real class—began to invade the town and offend its sense of inaccessibility. So the old power brokers decided among themselves to drive only three-year-old Ford or Chevrolet station wagons. The status came from *knowing* such cars were acceptable. In such circumstances covert symbols are born. They are used primarily to separate the chaff from the wheat. Only insiders are cued in; outsiders broadcast their unknowingness wherever they go. In this way members of the "good old boys" network identify each other.

In a large government agency, Amanda attended planning meetings every month, and every month she suggested a particular program which would not only make her work easier, but would also save the company money. But every month her suggestion was ignored.

One day, after Amanda had done a favor for an office peer, he told her if she really wanted to get her program accepted, she should announce at the next meeting "Mr. Abernathy has approved it." When she followed his instructions, her suggestion was adopted enthusiastically by the other attendees.

Later, Amanda discovered there was no Mr. Abernathy. This was simply covert code to signify the inner circle was amenable to the program. Anyone at the meeting who asked, "Who is Mr. Abernathy?" identified himself or herself as an outsider. Amanda, to her credit, recognized she owed a "big one" to her peer for sharing this information, even though it was a payoff for other favors.

MAKING CONNECTIONS

Aside from money, status, and information, the most powerful bartering tool is apt to be connections. *Who you know* is still the prevailing axiom, and for good reason. Life is a very dangerous game, and organizational or political structures simply mirror this fact. The bears are still in force, and teams still need people who are willing and able to negotiate their support and skills for the team. When one player is introduced to another by a third party, they all benefit, Nonplayers find such introductions hard to come by, since savvy men and women rarely want to present them as players. But, as with all power, connection strategies are flexible, depending upon the goals and skills of the players.

Ben lived in a relatively small town and had years before volunteered his time as the promotion director for the local chamber of commerce. One night he got a call from a reporter who had gotten his name from an old brochure. It seemed the chamber had invited Sarah Weddington, President Carter's assistant, to speak before the group, and the reporter wanted to know if a private interview was possible. Ben was sharp enough to recognize opportunity; he could certainly arrange such a meeting. As soon as possible, he contacted the chamber to get the name of the current president, called him and said, "I understand your organization has invited Sarah Weddington to speak before you. How would you like some coverage in a major newspaper?" The president was, of course, delighted at the prospect. "I can arrange that. I'll call you back," said Ben, who then phoned Weddington's office with the same offer. Weddington's aide was equally pleased with the possibility of a news review, not only for what it meant to her boss, but because an interview would signify she was doing her job in getting Carter's messages to the public. Ben assured her it would be handled. What he arranged was a lunch for four people—himself, the reporter, the president of the chamber of commerce, and Sarah Weddington. Three people were then theoretically indebted to him.

Brokering (bartering people) is popular simply because the payoffs can be so great. Aside from the obvious risk of standing behind individuals who prove to be incompetent players, the opportunities for personal gain are endless.

If a person interviewed for a job he was unable to handle, he can broker this position to someone else better qualified, and gain chips from both empolyer and employee. One can always call a member of any news media and broker someone who has information valuable to the public. John Kennedy met Jacqueline through a romantic broker by a mutual friend, who presumably traded their introduction for continued access to them when they were in the White House.

Virtually everything and anything can and is bartered. Two tools, however, carry more advantage than others, and they are available to people at the bottom of organizational structures. The first is the willingness to do the work and to trade the credit for it, in return for favors as yet unspecified. Kenneth Blanchard and Paul Hershey, in their book *Organizational Change through Effective Leadership*, point out the people on the *bottom* rungs of the company must be technically proficient and responsible for the development of the goods and services provided.

The beginning engineer needs to know how to build a bridge that won't fall down. The executives at the top instead need the political and conceptual skills to know which bridges to build, when to build them, or whether to continue in the bridge business. Nevertheless, as long as financial profit is made on bridge contracts, the senior people are ultimately responsible for getting and maintaining the bridge business. Stockholders want to know which vice-president is more valuable, which is less, and which is doing nothing at all.

TAKING THE BLAME
AND
WINNING THE GAME

The savvy comer barters his work for the benefit of those with responsibility. The inexperiened female, assuming recognition will get her approval and then reward, fights for her name on the exhaustive reports—and becomes known as a good report writer. Nothing else.

Nancy Fisher understood the power of her work far more than her coworkers who fought to prove the worth of their reports. She helped a neighbor complete a $100,000 computer equipment sale by using her position as a secretary in the local hospital to invite key people for dinner, to lobby for his particular word processor, and to set up expectations in the minds of the purchasers only her neighbor could meet.

She not only received no credit or recognition for her efforts, she received no money. The computer company does not even know she exists. But Nancy did get a payoff well worth her time. When she followed her husband to a new city, the neighbor arranged to get her hired in a company in which he had connections.

Trading credit for work is one side of parlaying responsibility for future favors. A more daring game occurs when the house is crashing down. Assuming responsibility for a failure, *taking the blame*, can also be used to advantage. In fact, there is no single action more powerful than taking blame, in return for, of course, favors.

A Japanese businessman came to this country to manage a factory in Ohio. After three years, he returned to his native land. But before he did, he wrote an article for *Fortune* magazine describing the difference between factory workers in America and Japan. In Japan, he explained, if a factory were on fire, the workers would run outside, gather in a circle and say, "Is everyone here?" "Who will call the fire department?" "Can we start fighting the fire ourselves?" "Where is the water supply?" "How about a bucket brigade?" and proceed to put out the fire. In the U.S., if a factory were aflame, the workers would run out, gather in a circle and say, "I didn't do it." "He did it." "I say him smoking in that section of the building." Meanwhile the factory would burn down.

There is great truth in this message. Lesser players at all organizational and political levels, spend an inordinate amount of time and energy avoiding responsibility. If fact it's estimated over 85 percent of all memos are in the CYA (Cover Your Ass) category. One need only look at the front page of any newspaper to see public officials blaming each other for the burning building while it is being devastated. The easiest way to gain immediate power is to say, "I did it. I lit the fire. Now let's put it out."

Sometimes he will be fired (and he can barter that too); more often he will be praised, rewarded, and protected. Why? Because the other fellows need him around the next time to take the heat.

Ron was a middling professional in a fast moving corporation where his boss was in charge of a very expensive program. It became clear the entire project was a waste of funds, headed for very visible failure. Somebody's head was going to roll. Ron's boss, Al, had three children of college age and didn't want to be the scapegoat. So he asked Ron to take the blame, in return for which... Well, Ron, had always wanted to attend law school. So Al arranged a full expense fellowship for his subordinate by cashing in a few chips with acquaintances on the university board. Ron confessed his failure, was allowed to resign with reprimand, entered law school, and was rehired by Al three years later when he had his degree.

Richard Nixon may have been president until the end of his second term in office if he had simply said a week after the Watergate break-in, "My people were overzealous and I am responsible; it will never happen again." We would have all yelled at him for a few days and then gone on to other distractions.

Taking the blame may be difficult to do when the stakes are high, but it would be surprising to learn how many people sit in prison carrying out other people's sentences. Powerhouses such as Martin Luther King or Mahatma Ghandi spent time in jail, responsible not only for their own acts but for the acts of their followers. At a certain level, as men say, it all becomes hardball.

UNDERSTANDING LOYALTY

The currency most valued by high risk power brokers is loyalty. There is a significant difference in our society between female and male loyalty. Women generally operate with what we call "marriage" loyalty. We will be loyal for ever and ever and ever, but only on condition that... (With us making the conditions). Men are more apt to use "football" loyalty; they will be loyal unconditionally, even unto death, but only today. Tomorrow the loyalty must be renegotiated. The guard for the Washington Redskins gets paid to protect his quarterback. But the day he gets traded to the Dallas Cowboys, not only does his loyalty go to Texas, so does the Redskin playbook.

When the bear attacks, the man alone is vulnerable. He must be able to count on human assistance, without having to justify or explain.

That kind of loyalty is hard to come by in anyone, but especially so in women. The authors know whatever one of us does—regardless of how badly she errs, regardless of whether her actions are acceptable to the other's value system—we will back each other 100 percent. No matter what. We know it because we fight it out over this issue twice a month, and neither has ever found the other wanting.

Our clients know the same. We understand many of them take big risks when they introduce us and our controversial Operational Politics program into their companies. So when they become clients we make a commitment to them and to ourselves: we *will* deliver. And we'll take the heat if trouble arises. We have lost important contracts as a result, but Aristotle Onassis was right. We can't afford to let it be said we are unreliable.

We women find this kind of loyalty difficult because it conflicts with our politics of judgment and exclusivity. At our seminars we're frequently asked, "How can you possibly work with someone you don't respect?" But if we begin to work with someone, we respect them enough to leave their values alone. We don't question their moral judgment or integrity. If we find that too difficult a burden to bear, we don't work with them at all.

To men of power loyalty is not optional. They don't have a choice. When Richard Nixon ran into trouble over Watergate, most of his team rallied together to support his stance, even though it meant jail. The alternative was to demonstrate to the rest of the male world an almost unforgivable unreliability. Those who stayed with him have been handsomely rewarded by Nixon and others who value loyalty. This is not rewarding collusion.

A soldier once pointed out he didn't know half the men at the conference we were attending, but anyone of them might someday be called upon to save his life, or he theirs. That is simply not a woman's perspective.

In reality, men barter for acceptance, trustworthiness, protection, and opportunity—all those things women used to barter in the home, and now demand for free in the office.

8.
Tribal
Roles

Because the bear fighting world is so dangerous most canny men operate in teams. Women are often accused of being poor team players. From the male perspective, it is probably true.

HOW INDEPENDENCE HINDERS

Female politics have always been individual, even in the cave. Such adages as "too many cooks spoil the broth" mirror the value of working on tasks alone. We have seen little need to join rank, influenced by our practice of exclusivity. Even when we try to unite, the union is apt to be of many women doing identical things together in independence.

Car pools, child care, and cottage industries all have common goals, interests, or needs. As long as that remains, and there is a moral commonalty, the female group effort continues. However, should one member of the group join another political party or try to bargain for a different share, the effort fragments or dissolves. There is usually a haphazard quality to women's collective efforts, not one of hard-headed realism.

But male prosperity originally *depended*—and still does—upon team play. As one bear fighter alone cannot overpower a grizzly, so one man alone cannot outmaneuver General Electric. Male team playing results from brokering and building a latticework of interdependent rewards and responsibilities. The goal is shared, the means are flexible. Nevertheless the team remains at the core. But it is not without purposeful strife.

Witness the complaint of the president of a growing computer manufacturing company who despaired of moving women into senior management. "Our field is rapidly changing," he said. "No one has a crystal ball into the future. We don't know whether to continue building home computers, increase our software line, switch to further production of computer peripherals, or start investing outside the field to protect ourselves against a possible shakeout. We don't know what to do to survive. So every six months, we ask our mid-level and senior people to prepare forecast budgets for company consideration. Eventually we receive 46 such proposals, 12 of them from our females."

"We then face another problem. We have narrowed the possibilities from infinity to 46, but each person proposes something different. We don't know whose view is the most advantageous to us, whose perceptions are the most helpful to the company. So we create a slugfest, wherein each official attacks, tears down, and sabotages the others' budgets while defending, advancing, and selling his own. The person who victoriously forces the others to adopt his goals gets to determine the direction of the company for the next six months.

"Whenever we use this process," he continued, "our women invariably refuse to fight for their budgets, personalize the attacks, and worst of all—refuse to wheel and deal around the issues. There are no women in our company who have the strength and moxie to lead." In other words, they won't play.

DEVELOPING TEAM ATTRIBUTES

Again, team play among men is illustrated best by football. Certain attributes and behaviors demonstrate team play and are essential in creating and maintaining strong teams. For one thing, team members have loyalty; they never tackle their own teammates. Football players wear uniforms to distinguish them; corporate players use code. The message is the same: don't badmouth or sabotage someone on your side, unless you've already signed with someone else. Women, however, frequently lack understanding of this basic premise. Our bent is to judge everyone so we know who to exclude from our circles. Voicing judgment is part of the process.

Good team players sublimate their personal goals to the goals of the organization. The fellow who has long dreamed of being a quarterback is ordered by the coach to gain 30 pounds because the team needs another tight end. He either does it, or he finds another team which needs a quarterback. That's the hub of loyalty. When a marketing manager loses a round to the operations manager, he doesn't sabotage operations. Rather he gets back in line and pulls with the team, all the while waiting for his next opportunity.

Team play also requires obedience to the coach and his objectives. Participation in a group effort under the guidance of a leader assumes the leader's mandate. A conscious decision is made to follow an accepted leader. It is not unconscious abdication of personal responsibility to impersonal rules. Team obedience signifies mutual acceptance of goals and willing trust in leadership that can create the wherewithal to achieve those goals. Blind obedience is unwitting and irresponsible and devoid of any connection to power goals. Teams require depersonalized cooperation. The ball is thrown to the person designated to catch it, not to the best pass catcher nor to a best friend. And more importantly, the smart male lets the catcher make the touchdown or fail, according his own actions, even though both may have to pay the price. An important team attribute is the ability to allow one's fortunes to rest on other people's skills and to be ready to take defeat with the rest of the team if one person acts imcompetently. This is how unified teams behave. Coaches get hired or fired on the basis of other peoples' behavior. So do managers.

The most important attribute of team playing is the concept of team roles, which is often difficult to accept from a female point of view. Among two people, only one is needed to make a decision. Among 2,000, only one is needed. Among 200,000, only one is needed. There is nothing democratic about decision making by sound leadership. It does not require votes, and when people insist on voting for an issue, it is a simple matter to stack the group with members who vote in favor of the leader's position.

Teams primarily consist of one or two *decision makers*, supported by team members who play significant but diverse roles. As in football, a team is a conglomeration of diverse but necessary functions which act in concert to achieve a common end.

The typical female concept of team play is to sit together discussing a particular issue or proposed action, then to vote—each participant ensured the others are not going to do her in. It is not in our general experience to follow the lead of another woman unless men do it too. We are, however, inclined to follow the dictates of a man, but under the terms of the hidden barter of security and comfort, not as a viable team member.

The most difficult concept for most of us concerns the roles of team players. We are so used to taking turns, we rarely understand the quarterback always plays his position with fame and fortune—while the tight end labors unceremoniously for half the salary and twice the bruises. But both depend upon the respective skills of the other to get into the Super Bowl.

THE MENTOR RELATIONSHIP

We often seek mentors to save us from the bruises. We want their all-encompassing protection. This is a common mistake. Mentoring is a power relationship of *equal support* between two persons of unequal rank. The protection is there, but it is bought and paid for under the mentoring system as elsewhere. In a word, the mentee has the same obligation to protect the mentor as she or he expects in return.

Mentors exist because there is a conspiracy of silence from those at the bottom against those at the top. Sometimes it is based on fear, other times it arises from true concern by senior executives. It is difficult for senior officials to get the information they need to do their jobs. And often as not, this information is gossip, not formal notes or reports.

Astute leaders create mentor/mentee relationships between themselves and some of their trusted subordinates. They barter information, giving the underlings news about the top which is unavailable to the masses; in exchange they garner news about the bottom. Mentees provide the gut-level data around which all organizations dance. Mentors groom underlings for interviews, help them make effective presentations, guide them on effective involvement with senior management, and generally strengthen their positions. It is this particular situation most women see and respond to, misunderstanding the quid pro quo relationship of protection. A mentor most often promotes a mentee as a team play which gives them all better leverage.

Mentors and mentees also barter loyalty, the bear fighting kind. The mentee keeps morale and loyalty high in the office when the boss is absent, and if the mentor is in danger of being fired, the mentees engender vocal support, threaten strike, apply pressure to the board, and use other cavalry-over-the-hill tactics to protect the mentor. Similarly, mentors fight for their mentees, claiming this was the first time, for example, the employee has sinned, and occasionally evoking those made-for-television words, "If he goes, I go."

Unfortunately, when women feel powerless, we act powerless. If our mentor's head is about to roll, we may feel terrible and wish it were otherwise, but more often than not, we'll sit on the sidelines and watch it happen.

At the same time, we perceive our mentors *should* protect us since we assume they have the organizational power to do so. It is another instance in which men generally will not trust us. Can we blame them? They will kill our bear, but can't count on us to help kill theirs.

In addition, when for reasons of discontent or disappointment, women leave the team, we usually shroud ourselves in a cloak of righteous indignation. This continues from our misunderstanding of the mentor/mentee relationship. Loyalty dictates only three reasons for jumping ship: "I am leaving for reasons of health," "I want to spend more time with my family," "I have accomplished my mission." Period.

This mentor/mentee loyalty takes a long time to create and is most effective when it is absolute. Both sides must be prepared to sacrifice their jobs, if necessary, for each other. That possibility is usually remote, however, since politic mentors and mentees don't depend upon just each other; they create a whole network of interdependent people.

An executive on the move may experience some difficulties when he is promoted if he doesn't leave a loyal team behind him. If he should be replaced by an ambitious young man, fresh out of Harvard University with an M.B.A., and eager to prove himself, the executive may find all his policies and procedures are questioned and changed by his successor. The smooth machine he worked so laboriously to install is apt to be dismantled by the upstart, who knows nothing and cares less about the operational politics in effect. Chances are the newcomer will try to carve out his own domain with the executive's formerly loyal subordinates. A palace revolt is apt to be the result.

The adept bear fighter will select his own successor, someone who has demonstrated loyalty in the past. In this way, there is a smooth passing of the baton and the executive still has access to his old team.

An ambitious man will find mentees throughout the organization, even throughout his industry. He will seek to place them wherever he can in his own company, in competitors', in the government, and in the legislature. The most plush positions are often bartered between two different power players of different teams, both of whom recognize the necessity of having reliable team members in key places. They both try to keep out the ignorant, who know nothing of barter and can only be manipulated.

CULTIVATING LOYAL ARMIES

The best mentee, of course, is one who has also created a loyal following below himself or herself so information gathering can be continued down the line without direct involvement. Female mentees who do not become strong mentors themselves are generally seen as "wives." While it is a comfortable role in its own right, it is not a particularly powerful one these days.

Richard Nixon's secretary, Rosemary Woods, and Mary Cunningham, a corporate vice-president, are examples of two women who operated as "wives" to their mentors. Both women focused their energy on only one powerful man; neither had an army of loyal supporters ready to move for her protection.

Loyal armies not only make team members more powerful for their bosses; they make them more powerful against their bosses if a parting should come.

One top executive explained Cunningham's popularity (she received over 200 job offers after her leave from Bendix) this way; "I've never had a vice-president who was technically talented and hardworking who was also expendable. Any of mine would take half the company with him if he were fired."

TEAM POSITIONS

Presidential administrations, like other groups which effectively work in concert, employ varying roles among the members. They just are more visible than most.

One obvious role is a *hit man*. He is the person who does the dirty work, fires people, and announces the bad news. He also shakes up ensconced systems, destroys complacency, and opens the way for power shifts. In the Nixon administration, James Schlesinger was generally known as a hit man. For several years, he was Secretary of Everything in the Cabinet, shifting from one department to another, removing "difficult" executives, reorganizing systems, shaking loose fat and sassy power brokers. Having accomplished his objectives, he moved on to do the same at another department. He left others behind him to build something out of the ruins he had purposefully created. Many presidents place hit men in every department, usually one step below the secretary. Then those two play "good guy, bad guy," and changes can be made without open revolt against the new senior official.

Some hit men make their living in just that role; they like it and are good at it. Others act the part for one position, for one day, or in one instance, depending upon the needs of the team and the organization. The advantage to having a separate hit man is sooner or later the masses will try to retaliate, and a moving target is hard to hit. The hit man can move on to another position or another company, leaving behind a team intact and relatively enemy free.

Women are rarely used as hit men for obvious reasons. A woman who relishes the role is considered extremely unfeminine by most who know her. Usually this attribute in a female is seen even by those who use her in this function, as a character defect, making her somewhat unreliable in their eyes. (Will she use this attribute against them?) However, some men like to use women in this capacity because we are fairly expendable and don't often know how to protect ourselves. Hit men can and often are sacrificed. Women generally do not yet understand how to extract the price for performance in this role.

Another well-known role is of the *front man*, a function increasingly in vogue because American voters keep insisting presidential candidates be communicators rather than decision makers. Some say Ronald Reagan is the "best acting president we have ever had." The person elected to the chief executive office of the United States is most often the person who *communicates* best, who can motivate, who can make us believe, and who makes a strong and purposeful appearance. Such talents are not the same as being able to create a vision for the future, set suitable priorities, create resources, or make tough choices—attributes which are also more essential for a modern political leader. Both parties tend to promote front men as candidates and to back them with decision makers who may not be visible to the public.

It is clear our national leader cannot make all the complex and far-reaching decisions for which his administration is responsible. It is equally clear the American public will vote only for an attractive and articulate communicator. The days are past when a balding, pudgy, bumbling accountant can get elected president. The divisions of power are so split they all take marching orders from someone else.

A *point man*, as any military person understands, is the one who draws the fire while the rest of the team is busy elsewhere. In our lifetime, the best point man was James Watt, former Secretary of the Interior. Whenever Watt made a controversial or outrageous statement, one had only to look back several days to see what Ronald Reagan had said or done. The week Reagan sent Marines to Lebanon, was the same week Watt was forced to resign over his remark: "We have every kind of mixture you can have. I have a black, I have a woman, two Jews, and a cripple. And we have talent." The sending of the Marines was an action most Americans were unaware of because of the hullabaloo surrounding the Secretary of the Interior. Good point men are often killed in the line of duty. So it was with Watt, although he was rewarded with the usual $500,000-per-year law practice or comparable consolation prize.

A *straw man* tests the waters and is usually put atop an untried project or principle to carry it to stability or defeat, then he hands it over to someone else who takes the credit for the idea. Some become straw men unwittingly and unwillingly, others are smarter. David Stockman was supposed to be the straw man for Reaganomics. When the President was first elected, his economic policies were largely untried and untested.

So Stockman was given public credit and responsibility for the theories and widely touted as the "author" of the program. If Reaganomics failed, Stockman's head could roll, and Reagan would be unsullied. If the program was a success, the President could and would take full credit for its development and implementation. However, few plans work the way they are meant to; in this case, no one counted on Stockman's extraordinary political sense and playing ability. The *Atlantic* published an article in which Stockman said he himself believed Reaganomics was a failure. He apparently hadn't negotiated taking the blame for anyone. All he had to do was to make the obligatory public apology, and the game went on. What backing he had, whose team he is really on, what personal consequences he had, we don't know. In fact, it's possible he published his article with the approval of the Reagan team, to allow the President to change his economic policy.

Women—and men—who personalize success and failure, who assume public praise is reserved for those who do good things, and public censure for those who don't, are obviously unsuited for this type of team work and behavior.

A *yes man* is a popular and misunderstood role in any organization; people often assume his purpose is to make the boss feel good. Untrue! The function of a yes man is to create a semblance of support for the boss' objectives and programs, just as the cue card with the words "laugh" on it do for a comic. If the leader is to announce a possibly controversial decision, he often brings along several yes men who work the audience to create support and to motivate individuals to jump on the bandwagon.

We used to suggest to homemakers when they wanted to impact community meetings, to go in groups of four, then split up at the meeting and make a pact that whenever any one of them said anything, the rest of them would immediately jump up from different parts of the room and say, "That woman is right." The effect was a sense of solidarity.

The difficulty around yes men is when the leader, so abused by hindrances, threats, and obstacles to his leadership, begins to believe his own press, and rewards those around him for playing the role spontaneously. The Shah of Iran, once more, is the result. It is too easy, with weak leadership, to settle for *appearances* of success in place of the real thing.

Strong leaders can detach themselves from decisions and programs which are no longer effective. They can detach themselves from the people who are tied to those decisions and programs. But being able to do this and knowing *when* to do it in an organization where priorities are placed on loyalty and teamwork is difficult. Some otherwise strong and capable power players simply cannot rid themselves of their loyal and supportive yes men when the time comes. It feels too much like divorcing a good spouse or throwing out dutiful parents or children.

Troubleshooters are often the leader's hired guns. They exist to protect him from going too far out on a limb where he could conceivably be sabotaged. As part of his entourage, troubleshooters stay close to home and often stand slightly outside of team play. Lawyers and accountants are classic troubleshooters. They can step in waving a mystical cloak of law or budget, and provide an exit for a harassed leader. Business consultants are starting to move into this positon where they bring their collective wisdom to the decision-making process. These troubleshooters can be anything from a formidable palace guard to window dressing.

A little understood role is of the *"no" man*, or *gadfly*, as he is commonly called. This person goes to the meeting and speaks against the leadership in order to measure the strength of opposition, the quality of the possible obstruction, and any plans against the proposed decision.

He reports to his team who and what is against their leadership. He infiltrates the ranks of the opposition, often leading (and thereby controlling) them. Sometimes the gadfly plays heckler. It is a common practice for speakers to bring along their own hecklers when they are speaking. Psychology is such that most audiences will automatically sympathize with the speaker against the heckler, so it is an easy way for the speaker to develop audience support. It, also, allows the speaker to quip those brilliant one-liners which make such good press. And if a real heckler emerges, the official heckler can badger the unofficial one and leave the speaker unscathed.

A more common role for women, and often an unwitting one, is of *scapegoat*. Occasionally, there is a situation when someone's head must roll in order to keep the game functioning well. Blame, as we have seen, can be an effective tool for increasing power, but it has its dark side as well. The gods that be sometimes demand sacrifices, and voluntary scapegoats play the role in return for rewards.

THE NATIONAL SPORT

The story of Anne Gorsuch Burford and the Environmental Protection Agency (EPA) provides an excellent example of the function of a scapegoat. When Burford first took her job, she appointed Rita Lavelle as the head of the Toxic Waste Division to enforce those laws. Lavelle decided to play win/win politics with industry and gave companies a grace period during which they could police their own cleanups before the government took them to court. At this point, the decision was simply a judgment call, for better or worse. Some environmentalists in the EPA, however, had been holding hands with industry on this issue during the Ford and Carter Administrations and saw Lavelle's approach as noncompliance with the law. Now these people, most of them liberal Democrats, wanted to get tough with industry and were already nervous Reagan was not serious about saving the environment. So they complained to their liberal Democratic friends in Congress who were looking for just such an issue to invalidate Reagan's policies with the public.

The Congressmen thereupon asked Lavelle to produce her files with memos, letters, and other data regarding her relationships with industry. Lavelle asked Burford for advice. She in turn, looked to the White House. The Reagan team saw Congress' interference as constitutionally forbidden when the country's founders separated the legislative branch from the executive one. Burford and Lavelle were ordered to refuse to hand over any documents at all. Both did as they were told, and both were cited with contempt by Congress. The game heated up.

Whenever Congress cites someone for contempt, it falls to the Attorney General of the United States to arrest and prosecute. In this case, the Attorney General was William French Smith, a close friend of Reagan. He refused. The game began to get out of control. Now Congress was faced with having to impeach the Attorney General. As the press was busy with its own game of trying to create another Watergate, the public was being drawn in to the point of no return. And it was in no one's interest to challenge the entire administration over what amounted to a minor point.

Commonly, when the game gets overheated, a scapegoat is found who will satisfy both sides, so everyone can walk out looking good. The scapegoat acceptable to both sides of the EPA situation was Rita Lavelle, high enough in the chain to make a point, but not first string on the Reagan team. Therefore, Anne Burford asked for Lavelle's resignation. It was not forthcoming. In retrospect, you might wonder why a team player like Lavelle would balk, but she had been under stress for months, and bone-tingling, mind-boggling, life-shortening stress causes people to do strange things. Anyway, Lavelle refused to resign, so Burford wrote her resignation for her and submitted it to the *Washington Post*. Then Lavelle personalized the events, felt defensive ("I've done nothing wrong"), and called the game by telling the press the resignation was not hers.

There was nothing left to be done but fire her and then choose the next in line to be scapegoat—in this case—Burford. That's how William Ruckleshaus got to be head, once more, of the EPA. Anne Burford was sideline to be used, for better or worse, as the team needed. Lavelle was convicted of perjury and—not having a team to protect her at the moment—went to jail.

Most teamwork is not formal or obvious, although there are institutionalized groups such as negotiating teams, representative teams (the United Nations), research teams, and ad hoc teams formed to resolve a particular problem. More often teamwork is sporadic, behind the scenes, and tacit.

But all teams have one thing in common: they do their strategizing at meetings before the meeting. Before every formal meeting or negotiation, individual members team up to plan their respective goals and roles. Sometimes women are invited to participate, sometimes not. Usually only those who are considered trustworthy attend.

Meetings before the meeting are only sometimes formal gatherings. They often take place in restrooms, on golf courses, at lunch, or behind closed office doors. Team goals, the "party line," and appeals for united fronts are some of the issues discussed. They are not pep talks, but strategy sessions called by whoever feels the need. Sometimes they take place serially, through a chain of phone calls, telegrams, or one-on-one talks. They do take place. There is almost nothing spontaneous about power plays.

THE HAZARDS OF BEING TEAMLESS

While this all seems time-consuming and cumbersome to the uninitiated, team membership is much less dangerous than operating without a team. Sybil discovered that fact when she was hired for a fancy job as contracts officer in a large electronics firm. She was hired by Bill, a man of rather wide influence and connection in the company. He himself worked for a vice-president commonly known as "The Frog." Bill and The Frog got along about as well as a mongoose and a cobra. They indulged in an ongoing power struggle. Bill had wider connections; The Frog had the CEO's and Board's support. Both were too experienced to snipe directly at one another. The Frog sought to undermine organizational confidence in Bill by attacking the competence of the people he hired. As the personnel department later informed Sybil, it was The Frog's habit to fire Bill's employees at the end of their three-month probationary period. Sybil stepped into this hornet's nest unknowingly, wanting only to do her professional best, proud of her reputation in the field and nine years' solid experience.

She handed in her work to Bill who invariably praised her. Just as invariably, it was returned to her later by The Frog, citing incompetence on Sybil's part. Every once in a while the Frog would invite her into his office to ask her how she liked working for Bill—a clear invitation to join his team. Sybil liked working for Bill fine. In fact, it was The Frog she had trouble with.

After three months, The Frog made his move to have her fired and sent his recommendation to the CEO, to Bill, and to Sybil. Then he went home to a heart attack and died in his bed. Sybil immediately requested a new evaluation, this time by Bill, who had never criticized her work. It was so ordered.

But Sybil and Bill had never established any loyalty between themselves. When he had approached the topic once, she had informed him clearly she wanted no part of office politics. Bill also knew he would lose credibility attacking a dead man (a real cheap shot among sporting men), and since he wanted to adopt

The Frog's team for his own, he agreed with his former enemy and had Sybil fired.

All thoughts about not playing office politics disappeared quickly as Sybil saw her reputation sullied and her job future jeopardized. As our client, she played "catch-up" real fast! She first had the incompetency report removed from her personnel file, by cashing in a chip she hadn't known she had with the director of the department. Then she prevailed upon the engineers she had represented in contract negotiations to get her a new position through their extensive network elsewhere. Sadder but wiser, Sybil has learned to play team politics with the best of them.

A network is not a team. Nor is a support system, which many women mistake it for. A man's network is the sum total of all those people with whom he barters. It is ever expanding among those of mutual interest and goals, not necessarily of mutual values and likes. They are the people with whom he does business, people who may join his team for some purpose, and others who may not.

The support system is most typically found back in the cave.

9.
The
Sexual
Factor

While much male political acumen stems from their experiences with the external world, male biology also effects political systems.

BASIC DIFFERENCES BETWEEN MEN AND WOMEN

There are undeniable sexual differences governing and influencing behavior. The first is women know who their children are. A female may be unclear about the identity of the father, but she knows she is the mother. No one can point to a baby and claim a particular woman was the child's parent. A woman knows if she is pregnant, knows if she gives birth, and sees the baby emerge from her body if she so chooses.

By contrast, men are dependent upon the word of women to inform them of their parentage. For all the ideas flaunted by fatherhood these days, it remains an intellectual acceptance for men, rather than a physical knowing. The acceptance involves the trust of females.

A second difference is the way children are conceived. A woman, in order to procreate, need only be present and alive. She doesn't even have to be conscious. At the basest level, a female does not have to be a willing participant in the sexual act; she need only be there. For a man to procreate, however, he must act—develop an erection, penetrate a woman and produce an ejaculation—all of which is risky.

A third physical difference is the man has his genitals on the outside of his body, while we carry ours protected inside. Somewhere before the age of three, every little boy discovers the consequences of this and learns to protect himself against attack on his private parts. He learns, specifically, to see "it" coming and deflect any blows away from his area of vulnerability.

Those physical realities create a political base in the male mind which has no correlation for the female. In particular, the idea of manhood becomes unalterably associated with risk. To be a man is to be a risk-taker. It is what he does to survive. Even if he does not grow up to become a macho hunter, he still learns how to take and manage risk.

Recently a senior executive in a large manufacturing company shared the fact he was very sickly as a child and didn't have the physique to challenge other young boys. The risk was far too great. So, instead, he learned how to negotiate with them for what he wanted. He was very proud of the fact he has never been in a fight or raised his fist to another. However, he ended his tale with this sentence, "I knew I had to do something other than fight, because I could not have won." He learned an alternative approach by which he *could* win among his peers. He was still operating on male principles.

A man at risk will increase his chances of winning as best he can. The little boy learns how to recognize and deflect physical danger; as a man he transfers this skill into other areas of his life, recognizing and deflecting danger on the battlefield, in the office, and at home. He suspects almost everyone and every situation until he learns otherwise. He prepares himself for danger before it comes; he trys to deflect it before it hits. A typical man does not trust another man just because the latter is his boss. Trust is a factor between two individuals, not something automatically guaranteed because of a station. That is why, even in war, smart generals do not send men to fight with one another until after some "basic training" where trust is created through common identity and goals.

By contrast, a typical woman will trust automatically until she learns, to her sorrow, it was a mistake. In the cave, we allowed access only to those we could trust and so we relaxed in our own environment. In the male world, before now, we relied on male protection—not only against bears, but against the predatory instincts of other men. Years ago we went out into public only with a man in tow, and we could flirt outrageously if we wanted because he would protect us if trouble arose. We knew he'd shield us from danger, because his station in life (our husband, our father, our brother) required it.

Male wariness is not just against potential bears, but also against women, because he is so vulnerable to us. He needs to trust our word if he is to establish any kind of family. It is no accident the totally loyal and totally weak female is many men's idea of perfect feminity.

Furthermore, he can be humiliated by us in the sexual act. We can fake an orgasm; he cannot. We can abolish his erection with ridicule, he does not hold similar sway over us. Physically and emotionally, the man in an act of love is weak. When the man is erect is when he is physically vulnerable—it is then he can be most easily castrated, and his enemies can gain advantage while he seduces the woman.

We represent another risk for him rarely discussed in polite circles. It was brought to our attention one evening, when a male confidant called on the phone. "How many times a day," he asked, "do women think about sex?" Not love, not a particular man who turns them on, just plain sex. "Twice a week," we replied.

"That's terrible," he groaned, "I'm at a meeting with some other men who are discussing the fact they all seem to want sex more than the women they know. For us, it's once every twelve minutes!"

Since this conversation, we have asked virtually every man and woman we meet to comment. The women report: "It's not twice a week, it's once a day." "Twice a day." "Once a week." "Once a month." "Never, unless I'm in love." "Never, because I have a man who satisfies me several times a week."

We hear from men: "Every eight minutes." "Twice an hour." "Once an hour." "Every time a woman walks by." "I love my wife, but I love thinking about the ladies more." Even if some men are faking their interest, as some women insist, it doesn't matter. Men apparently need to join rank over the "every twelve minute" declaration as the perfect male model. Women don't.

MALE HORMONES

It is not immorality that does this to men. Nor is it necessarily female beauty. It is testosterone, the mischievous male hormone which invades adolescent bodies and changes them forever.

The world knows a lot about testosterone. Scientists tell us it is the basis of male strength, aggression, and sexual urges. It peaks in young men around 20 and slowly diminishes throughout adulthood. That's probably why soldiers tend to be young; hard physical war isn't an old man's game. (That's also why a young marine we met on a plane confided he missed the drinking on a troup carrier, because beer "took his mind off girls.") Young women may also have their minds on young men, but they are more apt to be thinking of wedding bells and relationships rather than sexual release.

Organizations try to corral this aggressive urge in young men and divert it to their own goals. That is why most corporate training programs limit membership to those between 18 and 30. After 30 the male aggressive instinct slows. If a man isn't on his way up by then, he probably never will be.

What has *not* been researched, adequately, is the opposite trend for women. Instead of testosterone, women have estrogen, the female hormone, which regulates our desires. Chemists know estrogen builds slowly in women up to about the age of 35, when it drops rapidly until the female menopause. Estrogen creates sexual desire in women also, but it appears to heighten the nesting urge rather than aggression. Young women appear to possess an uncontrollable interest in relationships, whether or not we are married or have children. To love and be loved, to be accepted, rather than "to score," is our hormonal destiny. Probably this is why the need for approval governs so much of behavior when we are younger.

After 35, however, our needs seem to change. It is then women become less focused on family, children, and relationships. We turn our attention elsewhere; we focus on more global concerns and on abstracts such as profits. Young women don't seem to do well in active leadership roles. The Indira Gandhis', Golda Meirs', and Margaret Thatchers'—in contrast to other women—seem far more aggressive than the young. But aggressive instincts of older men pale in comparison to their youth. To produce equality of output, organizations might better limit their training opportunities to young men and more mature women.

The Male Dominant System tends to pattern itself after male reality. In so doing, it makes allowances for male sexuality even while it has tried to regulate it. Despite sexual harrassment laws, men still proposition women for a variety of reasons. Attraction and sexual urges do exist, even in the board room where all the attendees are masked in grey flannel pinstripes. We women often think we can hide our femaleness behind "correct" dress.

A senior official shared this story. His company had ordered a new computer system, and the manufacturer sent an attractive woman to his office to explain the machinery. Fourteen officials listened politely as she pointed out the idiosyncracies of the new hardware. They asked appropriate questions. They made helpful comments. Then they went into the bathroom and speculated on what she was like in bed. The official, mindful of his wife's recent reproof to be more honest with women, told this to the female service representative at lunch. She was livid, threatened him with a lawsuit, then declared, "It's only your dirty mind, not me. I dress and behave impeccably." The executive asked us in all sincerity, "Does she not know?" She does not.

The biggest problem our company has is convincing men that women honestly believe by their manner and dress they can control sexual instinct in men. Women have an equally hard time believing they *cannot*. We don't just think we can control their actions; we are convinced we can regulate male desire. If we are "professsional" we believe, the issue won't arise.

The men we've talked to find this so ludicrous and naive as to accuse us of making it up. "Why else," one asked, "would a woman spend all that time putting on makeup and fixing her hair if she didn't want me to be aroused?" We couldn't explain to him about the need for approval, he could have made no sense of it at all.

For some reason male bear fighters do not trust other men who are not virile. Consequently, men sometimes proposition women for motives having little to do with a woman herself. It must have something to do with the connection between aggression and sex, although no man we've talked to is able or willing to articulate it. An older man may begin to feel he "doesn't have it anymore;" he is in danger of being excluded and ignored by the younger men and by his more virile peers. So he makes obvious and noticeable overtures to women, often in front of other men, to prove himself. He doesn't want to go to bed with the woman, only to confirm in his mind --and the minds of his associates—that she *would* have intercourse with him. He wants to know he is still attractive to the opposite sex. This is why some men who are accused of sexual harrassment are proud of the fact and why other men don't ostracize them. Demonstrating virility is an age old (and old age) game.

PROTECTING REPUTATIONS

Those of us who grew up in the 1950s learned from our mothers the very worst thing to happen to a young lady was a marred reputation. Only nice girls could hope to marry well. The bad ones would have to fend for themselves. When Jinx attended a large university, she dated two young men from the same fraternity house. But mindful of her mother's admonition, she kept her virtue and reputation intact. Her sorority heard rumors the men kept a file on women who dated in their fraternity. But she wasn't worried; she knew how "nice" she was. One day, however, a sorority sister stole the file. Jinx was horrified to discover her reputation was as flawed as anyone else's.

Her mother didn't know men lied. When she furiously confronted one of her dates, he justified his sin this way: "You can't expect me to admit I didn't score when your other date said he did. I knew he was probably lying, because I know you, but the other guys don't. I have my own reputation to protect." And this was in the days *before* sexual liberty!

This game has nothing to do with women. Neither does the one where men use women to prove they are not homosexual. There is a need, apparently, among men to bear fight only with those of the same sexual persuasion. Heterosexuals only trust other hetero-sexuals; gay men only make loyalty pacts with other gays. Whatever the basis for this behavior, it is deep and relentless.

Years ago, a friend dated a young man who was an executive assistant to the president of a large corporation. He once introduced her to the corporate prostitutes...women who provided the test of heterosexuality for men with whom the company did business. If a branch manager from Peoria was being considered for promotion to headquarters, or if a contract negotiator from a new supplier wanted to make a deal, the gentleman would be invited to a party the night before decisions were made. If the prostitutes didn't score, the decision was always negative. Men only play with their own kind.

A modern variation of this sport occurs in a Northeastern company whenever a new man is hired. His peers invited him for lunch at Maizie's Diner. "We play a game," they tell the newcomer, "every time you touch a waitress, we'll give you a dollar. If you touch her where you shouldn't, we give you two bucks. And if she yells about it, we'll pay you five." The goal has nothing to do with women (although it would be hard to convince the waitress)!

THE FEMALE WEAPON

In spite of male hormones, when in comes down to the nitty-gritty, men will resort to war and women to sex. Sex is our most valuable commodity because men prize it so. But it is not foolproof. We know men kill, and they will kill us. When Ronald Reagan sends American troops to fight the Cuban soldiers in Grenada, he metacommunicates men will kill—in this context—Cuban soldiers. Who knows about the next context?

When women resort to sex, and we sometimes do, it is not in recognition of our own sexual urges, but of the power we hold over men. Many a male has tripped over a female skirt. Eva Peron virtually ran Argentina from behind her husband's shield. Whenever the Mary Cunningham story is discussed, most of the savvy men we know don't want to talk about *her*, but about how Bill Agee, a once powerful man himself, could be derailed by a broad. Wives are rightfully fearful of the sweet, young secretary who has replaced old Mrs. Grump. The gorgeous wife of a former U.S. Senator admitted she came to Washington to find her fortune by seducing the most influential man she could find. If men are ruled by their egos and gonads, then they must be in the same place.

Male vulnerability to female sexuality creates a natural bond among men which overrides many other considerations. Men join rank against a woman when male identity is on the line. Black men will join rank with white men against black females. Few black men have seriously objected, for example, to the myth Jesse Jackson was the first black to run for the Democratic nomination for president. Shirley Chisholm, a 1972 candidate, "was not serious, they contended."

Men will wink at the trifling faults of other men, although they will just as readily use a sexual misdeed against an opponent in a bear fight. A powerful male must sin against another man before his treatment of women is used against him. Thus, Ted Kennedy loses his driver's license over Chappaquiddick, while Wayne Hayes is forced out of the U.S. Senate for keeping Elizabeth Ray on the payroll. Hayes had, in his career, made a lot more Senatorial enemies than had Kennedy. Elizabeth Ray was only the stake on which they impaled him. So despite sexual harrassment laws and women's desires, "men will be men" and their systems will reflect this inalienable fact.

Many of the women who are not using sexuality are busy trying to regulate it away by creating a third sex— the professional. She is often an unknowing female variation of a eunuch: a member of the opposite sex who can toil without risk among the virile. But unless we are willing to become like machines, we have to recognize there is no third sex. We can either act like men, or act like women—or combine the skills of both. If we refuse to act like either one, we end up with nothing.

10.
Ready,
Fire,
Aim

There is no safe place in the world. Life itself is risky. Everyone wins and loses, sooner or later. The male world is even riskier for those who are not skilled in managing and minimizing risk. When a man finds himself witnessing an argument between his immediate boss and his mentor, he understands the risk. Eventually one of the men may turn to him and ask, "What do you think?" The one thing that is clear is he is not being asked his opinion. He is being asked to choose his team. Straddling the fence, blabbering, and responding according to the merits of the issue won't work, for both of his superiors will find this disloyal. There is no answer book in the sky to refer to for the best solution. The risk and consequences are unquestionable no matter which way he goes.

The cavewoman had some security about the size, shape, and function of her environment. Men did not. She could shut out some unpleasant conditions like the snow or the cold. He couldn't. She had no guarantee marauders would not burst into her sanctuary, but it was a sanctuary. He had left his. His protection consisted of his intelligence, his resilience, and his ability and willingness to join rank with those who would do the same for him.

A Male Dominant Society is not the safest place for women, but it is now the only option—caves have been replaced with office buildings.

Americans in general like their comfort—both physical and emotional. Our leaders have for many decades lulled us into believing life was getting safer. The populace didn't have to lift a finger; they'd be taken care of. To some extent, they have been. We are all recipients of new drugs, safer foods, lifesaving techniques, fire-resistant clothing, fine insurance plans, ski safety bindings, car seat belts, and other illusions of security.

We have paid dearly for this lifestyle—primarily in self-esteem. A psychiatrist attributes the drug dependency of modern youth on the desire of overzealous parents to spare their children the pangs earlier generations faced during the depression and two world wars. Young people, he says have been "spared" so many problems growing up they enter adolescence unable to cope even with mild crises.

THE OLDER GUARD

The older men in power today were products of the depression and World War II. Their resilience, self-confidence, and tough skinned approach to hard problems will be sorely missed 20 years from now. Those tempering experiences forged men whose goals were clearly defined, challenging, and critically dependent on bear fighting skills. Approval had little to do with it.

A favorite bear fighter of ours tells of an incident that happened when he was a young navy pilot stationed on an aircraft carrier in the Pacific Ocean. His buddy and fellow pilot missed his approach to the landing strip and blew up his airplane on the deck. Our friend was right behind him next in line to land. He had to quickly gain altitude and then get his emotions and thoughts under control within 10 minutes, the amount of flying time his fuel supply allowed. He couldn't just *try* to land correctly either—no excuses. Performance, not effort, counted. This is a man who understands the need to "keep his cool." He also understands the necessity for action.

Every option contains a risk. There are no risk-free options. The most comfortable option—and biggest risk of all—is to do nothing. A consultant friend insists everyone must "ready, fire, aim," to be successful. He admitted "ready, aim, fire" may be more effective yet, but most people engage in "ready, aim, aim, aim, aim, aim"...losing out completely. One of the best lessons children learn through video games is standing still will get them killed quicker than anything else.

She can't win the race if she doesn't enter. He can't hit the barn door if he doesn't shoot. He can't arrive somewhere if he doesn't start the car. To get across the swamp, we will have to risk wrestling a few alligators.

Charlotte dreamed of working for herself. When we co-authored a proposal, she became ultra shy about sending it out. "I won't submit it to the company," she insisted, "until I'm sure it's right." And she kept on reworking it, and reworking it. Of course it was never "right," for the only "right" proposal is one a company accepts.

Once women realize we're risking, no matter what we do, then we can prepare for it and lessen the chances we'll be badly hurt. Everyone makes mistakes. One of the biggest is to assume we are safe because we *feel* safe. The reason why con men, legal and otherwise, prosper is because they trade on their victims' feelings of safety. According to the *New York Times*, we are far more apt to be murdered by people we know than by absolute strangers. And yet because we don't *feel* the danger among friends, we often assume none exists.

THE BIG RISK

Usually the consequences we face are less than earthshaking, nothing that can't be corrected if we fail. However, most Americans, both male and female, put too much energy into avoiding the "Big Risk." We do whatever we can, even to the point of guaranteeing our failure, so we won't risk *making a complete and utter ass of ourselves in public.*

The American ego is in fragile shape. Most of us don't like ourselves very much. So we erect a variety of facades to protect our real selves from the scrutiny of the public eye. We obtain titles, fancy cars, expensive clothes, a professional demeanor, and other screening devices so few people will see the person underneath. Yet we are ever aware our guard may fall and folks will see us anyway. What a no-win attitude!

If a person decides to risk occasionally he will publicly expose himself foolishly. It will be humiliating, embarrassing, and painful. But not fatal.

If he decides to avoid risk whenever possible, occasionally he will still make a fool of himself. Human nature is faintly riduculous and we all get caught sometimes.

Shirley had a book contract with a major publisher because she led a large women's organization. This group was in serious financial difficulties, and Shirley decided to ask the publisher for a large charitable contribution. That way, she reasoned, her association would remain active and therefore sell more books. It seemed like a win/win solution for them both. She was completely convinced of the rightness of this idea when she heard this publisher give a speech on issues very dear to her group. He sounded as though he were totally committed to their objectives. So she made an appointment to see him, and for the occasion she brought along a laboriously created proposal for a large grant, complete with supporting data and high-level references.

When she entered his office, there was another person in the room completing a previous meeting. Their closing remarks signaled to Shirley the publisher's speech had been ghosted for the occasion, he personally did *not* agree with its conclusions, and he was not convinced there was a market for her book.

Immediately after the revelation, she found herself alone with the publisher. "Well," he asked, "what can I do for you?" All Shirley knew at the moment was it would be disastrous to reveal the purpose for this meeting. Wildly, she tried to think of an alternative. Her mind was blank. "I wanted to meet you because I, er, admire you," she blurted. "Thank you," he answered, "but why did you come here?" "Well, you're just such a wonderful person," she stammered, completely out of control and out of ideas.

The man was not dumb. He knew she would not have flown from another city just to say those things to him. "But why are you here?" he insisted.

There sat Shirley, making a complete ass of herself in front of the publisher. She knew if she revealed how much in debt her organization was, this man would pull her book contract. She was stricken with mental paralysis at the thought.

By the time she left, she had simpered, flattered, and flirted—pounding nail after nail into her own coffin—but she had not revealed her original purpose. Eventually, the contract was indeed pulled. When it finally happened, she knew her visit to the publisher had a lot to do with it. She could just imagine him discussing her ability to do media promotion.

Several years later, when it didn't matter anymore, she met the publisher at a party and reminded him of their meeting. They had a good laugh about it, even to the point of giving her some suggestions about what she might have done. "Why didn't you ask me about a particular obscure stamp or wine? And when I expressed ignorance," he said, "you could have apologized for confusing me with a major collector." His wife suggested, "Why didn't you make a pass at him? That he would have understood."

Later they met again, this time with his proposal that she do a book on a different subject. Humiliating oneself is never fatal, unless one commits suicide thereafter. As a strategy, it is infinitely preferable to humiliating anyone else. Rarely are such losses more than laughing matters later. With our tendency toward self-importance, we forget people seldom remember those seemingly awesome moments of humiliation.

The fear we feel has more to do with the lack of experience than the magnitude of the risk.

Fear and discomfort are part of risk taking, and accepting this reality keeps us from becoming irrational when they appear. The athlete who ventures onto the football field knows every time he plays, he risks being hurt, but he will get hurt only once or twice in his career. Taking the risk every day is the only way he can score a goal. Not all risks result in failure. In fact, few of them do. If a man finds he's failing every time he takes a risk, he's a masochist and needs a counselor more than a consultant.

Once he determines what risk he'll take, recognizing once in a while he'll lose, he's ready to minimize the chance it will happen. There are guidelines, but nothing works all the time and there are no guarantees.

There are several things men do to minimize risk—most seem outside of female experience. The first is to practice out of town before bringing the show to Broadway. One gentleman informed us the Kiwanis Club was created to give young men a place to practice power politics. Many men labor for years in staff assignments, out of sight, honing their skills until they are ready for the line and the limelight. Jinx never understood why many young lawyers and bureaucrats volunteered for thankless, nonpaying positions in community associations in the suburbs around Washington, DC, until someone pointed out these men were in training.

MINIMIZING DANGER

Team play lessens risk, but it does not altogether

eliminate it. Two bear fighters may be attacking the bear simultaneously from different directions. If one of them loses advantage, let's say he falls, the other protects him by drawing the bear's attention away from the fallen warrior. The individual guards the safety of the team by increasing his own personal danger. Thus is group integrity maintained.

Politically aware men do almost nothing spontaneously; they plot every move just as in football and war. Men *decrease their spontaneity*, especially when drinking alcohol. Our company has enormous difficulty getting women to recognize business social occasions are still business, not a chance to let down one's hair. We must constantly remind seminar attendees and clients of this fact. Men have confided they used to ply women with liquor for sexual favors— now they do it to get information a sober woman might not divulge.

Those men do not realize some women might tell without the assistance of a drink. The risk-minimizing maneuver of not disclosing anything unless one is forced to show his hand is not typically female. Our goal is to make men comfortable; theirs is to keep possible adversaries (including us) off balance.

Powerful men also plan for contingencies. If strategy one doesn't work, what next? They select, beforehand, strategy two and three. Our experience with women shows their reluctance to play the game is based upon their having only one strategy. When it fails, they are left high and dry with their private or public humiliation. When we prepare ourselves ahead with a variety of strategies ready to be employed by ourselves and our teammates many women become eager to play. A woman who says, "I only want to do my job," is admitting she has no contingencies.

INCREASING RISK
TO GAIN AN ADVANTAGE

Advanced bear fighters know how to increase risk in order to gain the advantage. Years ago, when Jinx was learning to ski at Stowe, Vermont, her instructor took her on as many intermediate slopes as he thought she needed. One day he took her to a trail she had not seen before. It was the steepest on the mountain. "Now you're ready for the big time," he grinned. She couldn't even bear to look down the trail, let alone ski it! "Sure you can do it," he said. "Just *lean down* the hill to get your weight over the skis."

While it felt like suicide, it was the right move. Most high risk maneuvers *feel like suicide* to novice players. Only the best poker players have the guts to increase the pot when they can't afford to lose. Good strategists bank on amateurs giving in because the risk is heightened.

At some point in high stakes bargaining, one's gut is worth more than one's brain. Men will, and do, switch from softball to hardball as the play continues. Women rarely have the stomach to continue.

A lobbyist told Pauline of accepting a positon as the director of a group lobbying for the right of nurses to obtain medical degrees by using their nursing training and experience in lieu of some formal education. He was then personally hit with 14 lawsuits! These were all filed by people he had never heard of! His attorney informed him none of the cases had merit, and all would eventually be thrown out of court. In the meantime, however, he would have to divert his time, attention, and money to the suits and away from the other issue. Whoever sued him hadn't like his goal.

The attorney later told us it is common for high stakes players to be diverted by challenges in criminal, rather than civil, court. If this seems appalling consider a picture which appeared in the June 3, 1977 issue of *Time* magazine. Taken during the Carter administration, it shows Griffin Bell—then Attorney General—and Joseph Califano—Secretary of Health and Human Services—laughing because one of them had presented the other a hacksaw for his birthday. Since both were being challenged in criminal court, who knew which might have to use it first they wondered?

Leadership is not a game for the weak. It is more apt to come to those who are prepared. Once a young child playing soccer was hit directly in the face with the ball. He fell down, screaming in pain. But the game went on. His father yelled to the stricken boy, "Play with pain, Jay, play with pain." We had never been told to play with pain. We're not sure what young women are learning on the soccer field today, but our guess is pain is not one of the lessons.

Finally, there is Mao's challenge; those who are willing to risk death will achieve what they want, for they will either get it or be dead. High goals are always accompanied by high risks. No one always escapes retaliation, retribution, or obstruction when he or she successfully imposes his or her decisions on others. The fabled fear of success afflicting many women is often fear of the negative consequences accompanying success.

Too often, we have been counseled fear and pain were signs of failure rather than the price of leadership. Applause is not a reliable harbinger of success. Approval is usually reserved for those at the bottom who do what no one else wants to do.

Young boys often play "king of the hill," where one child physically overcomes the others to get to the top. His reward? The others try to push him off.

11.
A Moral Necessity

It will take time. It will take pain and frustration and setbacks and fear. But it will happen because it is already happening. Every day another female begins to reject her previous limitations for the opportunity to be significant. Not on male terms. Not necessarily in the Male Dominant System. Not necessarily apart from it.

WOMEN DARING TO CHANGE

Another woman dares to think for herself—to reject the "shoulds" and "should nots," both of the feminists and the ultra feminine, the traditional and the macho, for a new vision of the future female of consequence, on her own terms. Still another decides to trust her own instincts. She relys on her intuition and own resiliency, instead of man-made security. And one by one, women will begin to heed a small internal voice that *knows*, it always knows.

And without a bang, without even a whimper,

women will begin to perceive themselves as savvy powerful individuals with female orientations, with womanly goals, with new feminine roles which have far more to do with priorities than with social approval.

THE NEED FOR TRAINING

The concept of teaching one sex the skills of the other is not a new one. Forty or more years ago, male management specialists discerned men would be more effective organizational leaders if they could employ not only the male skills developed through early socialization, but also the female skills of nurturing, listening, and caring.

Rarely, however, do corporate women have the opportunity to learn the skills which men develop informally as young boys. Perseverance under pressure, unilateral decision making, depersonalization, focusing on the goal at hand, team play, strategizing, risk-taking, bluffing, and similar skills are still a mystery to most women. Even when such skills are taught these days, (such as when young girls are encouraged to participate in sports) there is a particularly female focus which virtually masks the learning process.

Unfortunately, training is also needed to reaffirm female behavior. During the past 20 years, modern women have been taught to put down and degrade traditional female attributes so the young women groping their way through the business world today are equipped neither with the skills of the traditional male—or the traditional female.

For one client organization, we have developed a

course laughingly called "Geisha Training," to enable women to rediscover the feminine skills so effectively used by women throughout the centuries. As men can transfer the skills of the football field to the office without actually tackling one another, so women can effectively utilize their "wiles" in the boardroom without sleeping around.

As effective men combine female and male skills, and effective women do the same, the next step organizationally is to enable the two to communicate with one another. Words are not only heard differently by men and women, they are heard differently depending on whether the speaker is male or female. The woman who says, "Tell me what to do," is communicating something very different from "What are my marching orders?" The actual communication depends upon whether she is talking to a man or woman.

The conflict between dominance and submission in nonverbal behavior must be worked out, so women and men are not continually intimidating one another when one or the other steps "out of line." And finally, verbal communication within the overall context must be studied in metacommunication, using the same care taken in diplomatic circles. In fact, communication with one another—diplomatic training—is probably essential for both men and women in upper organizational levels.

THE ALF THEORY

Perhaps it is now safe to state men and women may have some naturally different goals. Herbert Alf, Professor of Psychology at the University of the

District of Columbia, promotes a theory explaining the differing rationales among nations. According to Alf, there are two prevailing value systems in the world—the Business Ethic by which everything is judged according to its profitability—and the Family Ethic, which focuses on whether or not a consequence or system is good for people.

A person operating under the Business Ethic perceives himself as successful only if he makes a lot of money. He buys a house in an area because he can sell it later for a profit. He sends his children to college so they can get good jobs. He needs to surpass the Jonses materially in order to feel important; he is impressed by expensive cars, luggage, and wine. He considers people who don't share his values backward. He may involve himself in a charitable cause to help others make more money.

By contrast, the person operating under the Family Ethic sees money only as a tool to achieve human benefit. That man buys a house in a neighborhood because it is a safe place to live; he feels successful if his family lives there unmolested, even though he may later sell the house at a loss. He sends his children to college so they will be better, more well-rounded citizens. He finds self-worth in doing good; his charity may consist of feeding the poor or getting doctors to volunteer services where medical help is nonexistent.

Women, by and large, still operate under the Family Ethic. As a group, we are still not motivated by the smell of profit. For us, money is still a means to buy family security and personal approval. It is still unheard of for a woman to jump out of a building because her stocks dropped.

Increasingly, women are being pressured to join the

Business Ethic for the sake of profit. The danger is, we will concede. But powerful women, under the Family Ethic, can fill a desperate void in the American political consciousness. Every corporate board, every government hierarchy, every political association, needs at least one woman of power to take care of the "people" values currently under attack by "the profit is all" thinking prevalent wherever men meet.

In fact, a safe guess would be powerful women may make better use of corporate people than indiscriminately moving them around the country, which destroys community cohesiveness, family stability, rootedness of young children, long range planning of schools, etc. They may look at the computer as a tool to increase, not only the profits of an organization, but also the quality of life of its employees.

HOW POWERFUL WOMEN CAN IMPROVE THE WORLD

Powerful women may influence government policy to create a welfare system which actually works. It was the male view of poverty that enabled Johnson's "war on poverty" to be profitable for the saviors while maintaining a steady supply of the poor to whom they administered. No committed mother could ever approve of a system which profited the professional nurturers at the expense of those they tended. (In families, such exploitation is called emotional abuse.)

Powerful women, in charge of psychiatric systems, may not tolerate procedures which keep clients and patients helpless, while their doctors become rich. Powerful women, influencing crime prevention, may recogize the connection between the fact most major violent crimes are committed by males under 25 years of age, and the increasing dissolution of the family and community.

Powerful women may influence education, legislation, and politics to create new perceptions of family and community—ones not dependent upon blood ties and wealth considerations, but rather upon the basic needs and economic welfare of people.

Powerful women may create a massive upheaval in education as it is now practiced in the United States. They may create more options for children of diverse needs, looking less at credentials and so-called job skills, and more at the real ongoing educatonal needs of people throughout their lives in this society.

Powerful women may do it differently. Left to their natural inclinations, they may not be as successful in creating wealth and profit. But standing at the side of those who do—and focusing instead on shaping organizational, community, and family systems that are good for people—they will make a significant contribution to the American way.

Traditional homemakers, alongside the newly termed Professional Women—and alongside secretaries, teachers, nurses, and other women employed in traditional fields—can strengthen family relationships and opportunities by eliminating the unnatural distinction between women "who work" and women who labor in the home. Furthermore, the work of the women "who don't work" needs strong critical analysis. God did not ordain that women taking care of children need also take care of dirt and cluttered closets. Or that they cannot transfer their skills elsewhere once the kiddies are grown. Or that they cannot make money when they need it.

It was the profit motive which took men away from their families, communities, and friends for most of the day, most of the week, most of the year, for most of their lives. Savvy women may find a better way to prosper.

Religion needs powerful women. Journalism needs powerful women. Politics needs powerful women. Crime control needs powerful women. Social services need powerful women. Child care specialties need powerful women. Medicine needs powerful women. Education. Advertising. Manufacturing. The Arts. Government. Industry.

The Military *doesn't* need powerful women. The military needs powerful warriors who understand how to fight and can commit themselves to doing it. It has been said part of the problems coming from the Korean and Vietnam Wars stemmed from a scarcity of superior fighting generals. After World War II, the American public and its Congress, sick of war and the inclination for war fighting generals often have, filled the Pentagon with good negotiating generals instead. Once the negotiations broke down, however, the fighting expertise wasn't there.

Generally speaking, women can negotiate better than they can fight. Our role is not as warrior, but as peacemaker; not in the Army but in the State Department; not on the battlefield but at the treaty conference table. There *is* a critical need for powerful women in strategic security councils, military oversight committees, diplomatic commissions, international groups such as the United Nations, and other organizations whose purpose is to promote peace and contain war.

When at last we dare, many women will take

leadership positions both formally and informally to inspire humanity to a better world, built not upon the foundation of money (and the greed and hostility money nurtures) but upon the knowledge humanity is the most important product, resource, and client on this planet! Women will be directly involved in both its quantity and quality.

Finally powerful women belong in the home, caring for children, the sick, the old, the community. It is probably here women need the most power, given the weakening in the last few years of our natural power base. There is nothing moral about being weak. It may be, in fact, unethical.

Lord Acton, the British historian, said all that was necessary for evil to flourish was for good men (sic) to do nothing. In the same respect, we believe it is morally unconscionable for women to do nothing, which immediately makes us morally liable for all the mistakes we have made or will make.

If there are 360 ways to view any situation, then those whose views differ from our own are not necessarily less moral or more evil. If we are to be significant, we must give up our propensity for judging and learn how to respect and honor our opponents.

And we must act.

The story of the Samurai Warrior was told to us by a karate instructor. He said it was useless to teach women self-defense. Females could learn the movements of karate as well as any man, he explained: even perform them with more agility and speed. The problem is, he said, he could teach a woman to gouge out a man's eyes, but she won't do it until she is 100 percent certain he meant her harm—and she can only be that sure after the knife is in her belly.

The Samurai Warrior, by contrast, was revered in the early Buddhist religion as a saint because he was willing to take upon his conscience the killing of an innocent to protect the many. Because he was willing to raise his sword against anyone, he rarely had to raise it at all. If he mistakenly gouged out the eyes of one who posed no harm, the Samurai Warrior would willingly pay the price, often death at his own hands.

Because such moral strength is lacking these days, true leadership is increasingly rare. We may not be able to emulate such responsibility, but we can seek it out and support it whenever we can.

There is a role for powerful women everywhere. Weak women are ineffective wives and mothers because they cannot control the resources and systems effecting their goals. Weak women in politics are easily and constantly exploited. And weak women in business are irrelevant.

In the final analysis, women, as a sex, do have a better understanding than men of what is important in life. But it is up to us to develop for ourselves the strategic mechanisms of power which will enable us to assert focus.

Until then, Jenny can't lead because the Male Dominate System forbids it and we tolerate the system.

Jenny can't lead because she hasn't yet the skills to influence and gain control in the Male Dominant System.

Jenny can't lead because she hasn't yet created the visionary goals giving female politics the advantage and creating a better world than men have produced.

Jenny can't lead because she's given up the Family Ethic and the only power base she can ever hope to have.

Appendix

TEST YOUR OPERATIONAL STYLE

Here is a quiz to determine if the leaders and members of organizations to which you belong are operating under the Male Dominant System. Use it also to evaluate the operating politics of the national groups listed later in the Appendix—or modify it slightly to critique yourself, your peers, and your superiors on the job.

Are Your Organizational Leaders:

1. Able to depersonalize failure and success without judging themselves or others?
2. Able to set significant goals for themselves and the organization?
3. Keeping focused on those goals without being upset by lesser distractions?
4. Able to drop unsuccessful tactics and substitute more effective ones?
5. Able to recognize and resist meaningless accommodation by others?

6. Able to sublimate personal goals for organizational ones?

7. Above judging and condemning leaders who disagree with them?

8. Strong, resiliant negotiators who can compromise and develop win/win solutions?

9. Able to focus and act credibly during periods of intense pressure?

10. Able to form alliances and compromise with adversaries without giving up principles?

11. Risk-takers who expect to lose or give up occasionally?

12. Women who can address the concerns of both men and women for mutual benefit?

13. Able to accept and communicate to people on all levels of perception?

14. Able to operate effectively together with divisions of roles, functions, and power?

15. Able to see all sides of an issue?

16. Willing to share power, credit, or blame in order to get the job done?

17. Able to plan contingencies, offer favors, call in chips, and otherwise operate in a Male Dominant System?

18. Respected and valued by powerful male leaders?

19. Mentoring loyal followers who give them clout in and out of the organization?

20. Considered absolutely reliable?

Do Your Organizational Members:

1. Judge their leaders by their accomplishments, not by their values, motives, or personalities?

2. Resist demanding guarantees from leaders?

3. Resist, rather than encourage or tolerate, obstructive activity in leaders or peers?

4. Back leaders to give them power even when values may differ?

5. Trust leadership to lead without demanding an explanation for every move?

6. Take responsibility for the selection of effective—or ineffective—leaders?

7. Select leaders with care and responsibility?

8. Pay attention to processes only as they effect ability to reach goals?

9. Understand and expect compromise by your leaders as an alternative to total loss?

10. Take responsibility for influencing organizational goals?

11. Resist denegrating leaders and adversaries?

12. Learn from the successes and failures of all others?

13. Allow leaders room to risk new strategies when old ones fail?

14. Recognize that men and the Male Dominant System are not the enemy?

15. Focus on organizational goals?

16. Demonstrate strong loyalties?

17. Support leaders under pressure?

18. Accept and execute team roles and functions to reach organizational goals?

19. Recognize personal and organizational risk in passivity?

20. Exhibit absolute reliability?

RESOURCES

Listed here are national networks and organizations representing hundreds of thousands of women. Some of them have great impact; others do not. It is suggested you use the previous quiz to determine which of them operate under the Male Dominant System.

American Association of University Women
2401 Virginia Avenue, Northwest
Washington, DC 20035 (202) 785-7700
  Dr. Quincalee Brown, Executive Director

American Business Women's Association
9100 Ward Parkway, P.O. Box 8728
Kansas City, MO 64114
(816) 361-6621
  Ruth H. Bufton, Executive Director

American Nurses Association, Inc.
1104 14th Street, Northwest
Washington, DC 20005
(202) 789-1800

American Society of Professional and Executive Women
1511 Walnut Street
Philadelphia, PA 19102
(215) 563-4415
Laurie Wagman

American Society of Real Estate Counselors
430 N. Michigan Avenue
Chicago, IL 60611
(312) 329-8427
  Lois Hofstetter, Executive Vice-President

American Women in Radio and Television
1321 Connecticut Avenue, Northwest
Washington, DC 20036
(202) 296-0009
  Phyllis Tritsch, Executive Director

Association of Girl Scout Executive Staff
P.O. Box 3000
Salem, VA 24153
(703) 387-0493
  Kathleen Genaitis, National President

Association of Junior Leagues, Inc.
825 Third Avenue
New York, NY 10022
(212) 355-4380
  Director

Business and Professional Women's Foundation
2012 Massachusetts Avenue, Northwest
Washington, DC 20036
(202) 293-1200
  Alice Gerlach

Caucus for Women in Statistics
Room 206, Rotunds
Natural History Building
Washington, DC 20560
(202) 357-1546
  Dr. Lee-Ann Hayek, Editor

Center of Concern—Women's Project
3700 13th Street, Northeast
Washington, DC 20017
(202) 635-2757
  Father Peter Henriot

Executive Women International
965 East Van Winkle, Suite 1
Salt Lake City, UT 84117
(801) 263-3296
  Mary L. Johnson, Executive Director

Federally Employed Women (FEW)
1010 Vermont Avenue, Northwest, Suite 821
Washington, DC 20005
(202) 638-4404
  Karen Scott

Federation of Organizations for Professional Women
1825 Connecticut Avenue, Northwest, Suite 403
Washington, DC 20036
(202) 328-1415
  Jeanne MacDaniels

General Federation of Women's Clubs
1734 N Street, Northwest
Washington, DC 20036
(202) 347-3168
  Jeri Winger, President

International Association for Personnel Women
5820 Wilshire Boulevard
Los Angeles, CA 90036
(213) 937-9000
  Jean Replogle

League of Women Voters
1730 M Street, Northwest
Washington, DC 20036
(202) 429-1965
  Dorothy Ridings, President

National Association for Female Executives
1041 Third Avenue
New York, NY 10021
(212) 371-0740
  Wendy Rue, Executive Director

National Association for Women Deans, Administrators, and Counselors
1325 18th Street, Northwest, Suite 210
Washington, DC 20036
(202) 659-9330
  Dr. Patricia Rueckel

National Association of Bank Women
500 North Michigan Avenue, Suite 1400
Chicago, IL 60611
(312) 661-1700
  Phyliss M. Haeger, Executive Vice-President

National Association of Insurance Women
1847 East 15th Street, P.O. Box 4410
Tulsa, OK 74159
(918) 744-5195
  Mary Lynn Claiborne, Executive Director

National Association of Media Women
1185 Niskey Lake Road, Southwest
Atlanta, GA 30221
(404) 344-5862
  Xernona Clayton Brady, National President

National Association of Negro Business and
Professional Women's Clubs
1806 New Hamphsire Avenue, Northwest
Washington, DC 20009
(202) 483-4206
  Frankie Jacob Gillette, National President

National Association of Women Business Owners
500 North Michigan Avenue, Suite 1400
Chicago, IL 60611
(312) 661-1700
  Sandra Cook, Executive Director

National Association of Women Lawyers
1155 East 60th Street
Chicago, IL 60637
(312) 947-3549
  Patricia O'Mahoney, Secretary

National Forum for Executive Women
1101 15th Street, Northwest
Washington, DC 20005
(202) 331-0270
  Mary E. Neese, Director

National Order of Women Legislators
2607 Kona Lane
Anchorage, AK 99503
(907) 243-143
(907) 243-1459
  Thelma Buchholdt, Treasurer

NOW (National Organization for Women)
1401 New York Avenue, Northwest, Suite 800
Washington, DC 20005-2102
  Judy Goldsmith, President

National Woman's Party
144 Constitution Avenue, Northeast
Washington, DC 20002
(202) 546-1210
  Elizabeth Chittick, President

National Women's Education Fund
1410 Q Street, Northwest
Washington, DC 20009
(202) 462-8606
  Becky Bond, Program Manager

National Women's Political Caucus
1275 K Street, Northwest, Suite 750
Washington, DC 20005
(202) 898-1100

National Women's Studies Association
University of Maryland
College Park, Maryland 20742
(301) 454-3757
  Carol Combs, Coordinator

Pi Lambda Theta
4101 East Third Street
Bloomington, IN 47401
(812) 339-3411
  Dr. Jacquelyn H. McCullough, Executive Director

Professional Secretaries International
2440 Pershing Road, Suite G10
Crown Center, Kansas City, MO 64108
(816) 474-5755
    Jerome A. Heitman, Executive Director

Women Executives in State Government
1730 Rhode Island Avenue, Northwest, Suite 1012
Washington, DC 20036
    Meg Armstrong, Executive Director

Women in Communications
P.O. Box 9561
Austin, TX 78766
(512) 345-8922
    Mary Jane Kolar, CAE, Executive Director

Women in Telecommunications
109 Minna Street, Suite 298
San Francisco, CA 94105
(415) 564-8717
    Constance Beutel, Director, National Board

Women Library Workers
2027 Parker
Berkeley, CA 94704
(415) 540-6820
    Carol Starr, National Coordinator

Women Life Underwriters Conference
1922 F Street, Northwest
Washington, DC 20006
(202) 331-6049
    Liane Gonzalez, President

Women Officials in NACO
440 First Street, Northwest
Washington, DC 20001
(202) 393-6226
  Roxi Nicolson

Women's Action Alliance
370 Lexington Avenue
New York, NY 10017
(212) 532-8330
  Sylvia Kramer, Executive Director

Women's Bureau Constituents
c/o Women's Bureau
Department of Labor
200 Constitution Avenue, Northwest
Washington, DC 20210
(202) 523-6611
  Dr. Leonar Cole Alexander

The Women's College Coalition
1725 K Street, Northwest, Suite 1003
Washington, DC 20006
(202) 466-5430
  Marcia Sharp, Executive Director

Women's Council of Realtors
430 North Michigan Avenue
Chicago, IL 60611
(312) 329-8483
  Catherine Collins, Executive Vice-President

Women's Equity Action League
1205 E Street, Northwest, Suite 305
Washington, DC 20005
(202) 898-1588
    Char Mollison, Executive Director

Women's National Book Association
H.W. Wilson Company
950 University Avenue
Bronx, NY 10452
(212) 588-8400 (Ext-257)
    Cathy Rentschler, Secretary

Women USA
76 Beaver Street
New York, NY 10005
(212) 422-1414
    Bella Abzug, President

Women's Workforce
c/o Wider Opportunities for Women
1325 G Street, Northwest, LL
Washington, DC 20005
    Cynthia Marano

Zonta International
35 East Wacker Drive
Chicago, IL 60601
(312) 346-1445
    Valerie F. Levitan, Executive Director

ADVOCATES OF THE MALE DOMINANT SYSTEM

The following is a list of people who have taken one or more of Operational Politics Inc.'s courses and have found the concepts presented there—and in this book—to be true. They can be contacted for more information on OPI and how the principles have worked for them.

Jenny Beach
8427 Snowden Oak Place
Laurel, MD 20708
(301) 776-3605

Judi Carroll
P.O. Box 5000
Del Mar, CA 92014

Gayle Costanzo
12161 Wilsey Street
Poway, CA 92064
(619) 748-7412

Evelyn Day
Department of Commerce
Room 6012, 14th Street
Washington, DC 20230
(202) 377-0625

Mike Driver
1610 Emerson Street
Denver, CO 80218
(303) 832-2372

Martha Dohring
9 Los Coyotes Drive
Pomona, CA 91766
(714) 622-2697

Kathy Duffy
383 A Explorer Court
Grand Junction, CO 81506
(303) 242-5080

Sharry Fhite
1415 A Wright Circle
Washington, DC 20036
(202) 574-3212

Shari Flatt
743 Ash Drive
Grand Junction, CO 81501
(303) 243-7667

Karen Hastings
2908 Morningside Drive
Tallahassee, FL 32301
(904) 656-2533

Joan Humphries
14206 Day Farm Road
Glenelg, MD 21737
(301) 854-6023

Jean Kerr
8215 Carleigh Park Lane South
Springfield, VA 22152
(703) 569-9633

Patty McCracken
16 Glengyle Lane
Sterling, VA 22170
(703) 430-8929

Lynne Dominick Novack
1680 S. Elwood
Street Tulsa, OK 74119
(918) 585-5040

Lori Pinello
709 Orion
Colorado Springs, CO 80907
(303) 635-4733

Billi Ramsberger
3145 S. Lafayette Street
Englewood, CO 80110
(303) 781-3202

Cindy Taubber
3403 Marble Oak Court
College Park, MD 20740
(301) 763-7553

Mary Walton Yost
1958 Sunset Strip Blvd #196
San Diego, CA 92107
(619) 222-4792

OPERATIONAL POLITICS, INC (OPI) was created to promote the understanding and effective use of organizational power. To that end, the company has developed the following products:

BASIC OPERATIONAL POLITICS FOR WOMEN: a 2 1/2 day program open to the public or developed for individual organizations.

BASIC OPERATIONAL POLITICS FOR MEN AND WOMEN: a 2 1/2 day program for young men and women with technical expertise. Open to the public. Programs also developed for individual organizations.

ADVANCED OPERATIONAL POLITICS: open only to graduates of OPI BASIC programs.

"MEN, WOMEN, AND BEARS": a twenty-five minute videotape on the operational difference between men and women. Workbooks are available for use as a training tool.

"OPERATIONAL POLITICS IN BRIEF": a set of six cassette tapes on the major concepts of OPI.

OPI CONSULTATION AND NEGOTIATION SERVICES: Services and additional training programs designed to meet individual and organizational needs.

OPI INSTITUTE FOR WOMEN: a two to six week "total immersion" training for women who are seriously career minded (to begin in 1986).

OPI PERSONNEL SERVICE: an organizational service to help managers identify and employ women with political savvy (to begin in 1986).

For further information, please contact:

OPERATIONAL POLITICS, INC.
P.O. Box 9173
Grand Junction, Colorado 81501
303 243-8949.

- Give a copy of this book to a friend!
- Share it with your business associates!
- Use it for fund raising in women's groups!

ORDER COUPON

YES, I want to invest $10 in my future!

Send _____ copies of *Why Jenny Can't Lead: Understanding the Male Dominant System*. Please add $2.00 postage and handling per book. (Colorado residents add $.30 sales tax.) Note: Canadian orders must be accompanied by a *postal money order in U.S. funds*. Allow 30 days for delivery.

_____ Check or money order enclosed

Please charge my _____ Visa _____ Master Card

　　　　Account # _____ Exp. Date _____

　　　　Signature _____

Name _____

Occupation _____

Address _____

City/State/Zip _____

Please make your check payable to:

Communication Creativity
P.O. Box 213, Saguache, CO 81149
303 589-8223 or 303 655-2504

Bulk Inquiries Invited